THE VICTORIAN AND EDWARDIAN SEASIDE

THE VICTORIAN AND EDWARDIAN SEASIDE

JANICE ANDERSON
EDMUND SWINGLEHURST

COUNTRY LIFE BOOKS

Published by Country Life Books
and distributed for them by
The Hamlyn Publishing Group Limited
London . New York . Sydney . Toronto
Astronaut House, Feltham, Middlesex, England

First published 1978
ISBN 0 600 39143 4

Designer: Gail Rose

Phototypeset in England by
Keyspools Limited, Golborne
Printed in England by
Cox & Wyman Limited, Fakenham

Contents

Discovering the Sea

ON 30 July 1847, Her Majesty Queen Victoria wrote in her diary: 'Drove down to the beach with my maid and went into the bathing machine, where I undressed and bathed in the sea (for the first time in my life), a very nice bathing woman attending me. I thought it delightful until I put my head under the water, when I thought I should be stifled.'

Queen Victoria was not the first royal bather, for George III had bathed at Weymouth to the accompaniment of a chamber orchestra and George IV had been dipped in the sea at Brighton by that redoubtable bathing woman Martha Gunn. One might claim, however, that she was the first monarch to bathe for the fun of it rather than from a desire to improve her health, and by doing so she was keeping up with her times.

During the mid-nineteenth century the seaside resorts began to lose their character of substitute spas and became holiday places where the pursuit of pleasure was more important than the cultivation of good health. The process which had begun when steamer transport became available at economic prices between large cities and the nearby seaside, was accelerated by the establishment of the railways.

At first, most newcomers to the seaside watering places arrived only for the day, like a horde of invading ants. They upset the leisured middle-class residents who had set up villas by the sea in which to enjoy its health-giving air and engage in a social life which emulated that of the spas at the height of their fashion, but they did not overwhelm them. It was only a matter of time before they did so.

The seaside of the leisured classes had grown out of the spa habit and the transition from inland spa to sea had been gradual. It had begun at Scarborough, where a mineral spring by the seashore had first attracted visitors to the town. A few enthusiasts bathed there in the seventeenth century when the government had even considered taxing bathers on the grounds that the sea belonged to the kings of England. A few aristocrats sporting themselves, usually naked, in the sea were not enough to create a trend and it was not until the decay of the spas that seaside resorts became more popular.

Their popularity was given an impetus in the mid-eighteenth century by the work of Dr Richard Russell, who set about promoting the use of seawater to cure disease with the enthusiasm and determination of any modern-day public relations expert. According to Russell, seawater taken internally in half-pint doses, mixed if necessary with port or milk, could cure scurvy, jaundice, gonorrhoea, gout and other diseases. The fashion for seaside holidays having been established, the visitors set about creating the same atmosphere that had prevailed at the inland spas. Assembly rooms were built, establishments for taking the waters and, later, bathing in them, were set up by doctors and professors of the new science, reading rooms were built at which card games and raffles were included among the amusements and, as at the spas, every social event was designed to provide a medium for getting to know other visitors.

This kind of life depended for its successful operation on the approximate social equality of those who took part. When the railways arrived the seaside received a rude shock. No longer were the residents of the seaside watering places a select company cocooned in their private world. Suddenly hordes of people of all descriptions began to arrive on the scene and alongside the villas there sprang up the houses of tradesmen and boarding-house keepers who provided the services required by the new visitors to the resort. Moreover, with the new visitors there came new forms of entertainment and catering. Street musicians, minstrel shows, acrobats, whelk stands, ice cream carts, itinerant photographers, and pedlars swarmed about the quiet resorts turning the beach and promenades into a fairground.

Some resorts, either because they did not get a railway

or because they resisted any attempt to improve communication with large industrial towns, or because they were not suitable for development, remained small and picturesque. The rest of them grew and developed into highly organised towns with properly regulated local services which provided housing, transport, lighting, sanitation and all the amenities needed to satisfy the demands of the increasing number of residents and visitors. By 1900, after centuries of indifference, the coasts of Britain had become populated with hundreds of towns and villages where once there had been only a few fishermen's cottages or empty cliffs.

But what was the cause of this rapid change of attitude towards the sea? As in so many other aspects of social change in the nineteenth century the answer must be looked for in the changing circumstances of the population. The imprisoning of a previously rural population in industrial towns from which, until the establishment of the railways, escape was almost impossible, aroused strong subconscious desires for freedom. This urge was well expressed by the habit of absenteeism on Mondays, the excessive drinking and gambling, the crime and violence which frustration bred.

In these circumstances the seaside provided many avenues of escape, and the sea itself, vast, moody, provided the scene for the projection of intangible subconscious desires. It is unlikely that many of those who sat on the beach were ever much aware of this, although to some, like Charlotte Brontë who fainted at her first encounter with it, the ocean expressed the romantic spirit of the age. To others caught up in the religious fervour of the time, the sea was a symbol of God's might and to yet others it was a constant reminder of Britain's growing power gained by the exploits of her Navy.

To everyone the sea was a place where social life and social pleasures were the goal. In a class-ridden society one of these pleasures was the knowledge that one was emulating one's superiors.

The status of visitors who stayed at resorts was a recommendation for the place and an attraction for the visitor. In this game, kings, queens, princes and princesses were trump cards but almost any member of the aristocracy would do. Lists of visitors at a resort were published in the local newspapers, some of which owed their existence to the demand for publications in which visitors' names could appear. In Southport the paper was actually called THE VISITER. One can imagine how avidly the columns were read and with what envy it was discovered that a social rival at home was staying at the Grand Hotel. Snobbery was not limited to the upper and middle classes; even those without pretensions to status joined in the game of hunting celebrities or trying to identify them as they rode in their carriages up and down the parade, or strolled along the esplanade after church.

Lyme Regis about 1850. The small Dorsetshire town was not so very different at this time from the watering place to which the Earl of Chatham had taken his sick younger cousin, William Pitt, or to which Jane Austen took the characters of her novel *Persuasion*.

Serendip, Lyme Regis

About 1850

Lyme Regis, from the Pierhead

As the century drew on the popular crowds increased, the smart people moved away, and the newspapers gave up carrying lists of visitors and turned their attentions to discussion about different systems for dealing with sewage and reporting on such popular amusements as the Pierrots, the black-faced minstrels and incidents on the piers, which were now the status symbol of every resort.

9

The selective character of the social scene, the balls at which a master of ceremonies acted as host, much in the way that Nash had once done at Bath, meant nothing to the new visitors to the seaside. What appealed to them about seaside resorts was the fact that on the promenade and beach social differences passed unnoticed in a way which would have been impossible at a spa where everyone knew everyone else. The tradesman and his wife at their boarding house might know their place where circumstances demanded it but on the beach they could carry on in whatever way they chose.

This, too, was a kind of freedom which gave the seaside a strong appeal and which gradually broke down the prim attitudes of middle-class Victorian society.

On the beach the men and women of the working class with their less sophisticated and more frank sensuality behaved in a manner which shocked the more genteel middle-class visitor and drove the more sensitive ones to undeveloped villages in the west of England and Wales or abroad.

It was inevitable too that sexuality should be more openly pursued by the sea. The young men peered through telescopes at the women descending into the sea from their machines and the women let their hair hang wild and loose after their bathe and wore special corsets for healthy posture which by coincidence also raised the bust and thrust out the bottom in a provocative curve. It was no accident that the postcard whose theme is sexual humour should have developed at the seaside.

In a world in which the constraints of society grew more and more trying, the seaside called to the wilder nature of the beings who dressed in sober hues and mouthed only the most righteous platitudes. On the shores of Britain was another world of time and space. Even the architecture took on a more exotic style and in the winter gardens tropical plants provoked romantic images of the jungle. Here the dull, workaday world could be put aside for a week or two and replaced by a world of fantasy. It was this other-world quality which gave, and still gives, the seaside its strongest appeal. For in the seaside world fancy could roam among the Pierrots and minstrels and acrobats and, like a view of the front through the camera

Facing page
Before the railway, Blackpool was served by stage-coaches, such as the Omnibus called 'Safety', which took eight hours to do the forty-mile journey from Colne to Blackpool. A year after this advertisement was printed, the railway reached Blackpool, and the era of the stage-coach was over.

obscura, everything seemed brighter than reality. In its evolution the seaside became the world's most glamorous stage on which all who visited it could play whatever rôle they fancied for a brief space of time.

Sea Bathing.

The Public are respectfully informed that an OMNIBUS called

THE SAFETY

Will commence Running to the SIMPSON'S HOTEL.

BLACKPOOL,

On Wednesday, the 21st May, 1845,

From the HOLE IN THE WALL INN, in COLNE,

And from the OLD RED LION INN, BURNLEY,

Through Blackburn, Preston, and Lytham to Blackpool Three Times a Week, viz.—

On Wednesdays and Fridays from Colne, starting at Six o'clock in the Morning, and leaving Burnley at Seven o'clock, and reaching Blackpool at Two o'clock in the Afternoon, and on Monday Mornings from Burn'ey at Seven o'clock.

The above Omnibus will leave Blackpool returning to the above places every Tuesday, Thursday, and Saturday, at Ten o'clock in the Forenoon.

N. B. Arrangements will be made so that Passengers will be able to proceed through to Blackpool, without stopping except for change of Horses.

PERFORMED BY THE PUBLICS MOST OBEDIENT SERVANTS.

STUTTARD, ALLEN, & Co.

H. EARNSHAW, PRINTER, COLNE.

Above
In the 1850s ladies who bathed at Ilfracombe had a
private beach, reached through a tunnel in the
rocks, and provided with its own bathing machines.

Right
Sidmouth at the beginning of Victoria's reign was
still a very simple resort, despite having achieved
a short-lived popularity because of a visit by
George III in 1791.

Above, top
Daddyhole Cove and the cliffs to the east of
Torquay were a secluded area dominated by a few
large mansions for much of Victoria's reign.

Above
Ladies bathing at Brighton in the 1850s had to put
up with being stared at by fresh young men armed
with spy glasses—a nuisance common to most of the
popular resorts.

Left
Although Shanklin, Isle of Wight, remained a small secluded resort until the twentieth century, it had quite early in the nineteenth century several of the amenities to be found in the larger mainland resorts, including public baths.

Below
Dr Mahomed's Baths at Brighton was a popular source of medicated baths and massages in the first part of Victoria's reign, but later establishments such as Brill's Swimming-Bath for Ladies and an increasing preference for seabathing put Dr Mahomed's Baths out of business. The building became Markwell's Royal Hotel.

MAHOMED'S BATHS.

Above
Phiz, the illustrator of many of Charles Dickens' books, drew this picture of ladies exercising their horses on the beach at Brighton.

Right
By the end of the Edwardian period, resorts were competing fiercely for visitors. Torquay made much of the fact that Ruskin had dubbed the town 'the Italy of England', and Scarborough always advertised herself as 'The Queen of the Watering Places'. In this advertisement, the town is also highlighting an innovation – 'bathing bungalows'.

Facing page, top
Bathing at Scarborough in the 1850s. The girls in their flannel shifts are being watched over by a bathing woman.

Facing page, bottom
Victorians at the seaside: a crowded beach with pedlars, donkeys, bathing machines and wooden spades.

SCARBOROUGH

The Children's Paradise.

Enjoyment for ALL.

SOUTH BAY, SCARBOROUGH.   [Photochrom Co.

THE QUEEN OF WATERING PLACES.

BRIGHT, EXHILARATING, AND HEALTHY.   RICH IN NATURAL BEAUTIES.

THE FINEST MARINE DRIVE IN EUROPE.

CLARENCE GARDENS AND QUEEN'S PARADE.

BEAUTIFUL GARDENS BY THE SEA.

Latest Innovation – BATHING BUNGALOWS.

A CONVENIENT CENTRE FOR TOURISTS.   SEA AND MOORLAND AIR.

EXCELLENT TRAIN SERVICE

from all parts during the Summer Season.   Through Carriages from

Birmingham, Bristol, Derby, Leamington, London, Liverpool, Leicester, Manchester, Northampton, Nottingham, Oxford, Rugby, Southampton, and all the large towns of Yorkshire.

An Illustrated Booklet containing description of Scarborough and lists of Hotels, Boarding and Lodging Houses sent post free on application to the Town Clerk, Town Hall Buildings, Scarborough. For further particulars, apply to Thos. Cook & Son.

MUSIC, ENTERTAINMENTS, PROMENADES, BOATING, FISHING, 3 GOLF COURSES, 20 TENNIS COURTS, 5 BOWLING GREENS, MODERN BATHING FACILITIES.

ROCK & Cº
LONDON

March 31st 1857

DOWN AT THE SEA SIDE

A Ticket to the Seaside

HAD it not been for the invention of transport which could carry large numbers of passengers at low cost the seaside resorts, as we know them today, might never have got going.

Before the steamers and railways, the seaside was a place for the rich who built or rented private villas and travelled to them for a long stay, usually in the wintertime. The introduction of steamer services from large inland cities and towns to the fishing villages and ports along a nearby coast brought on radical change which became ever more widespread when the railway arrived.

Among the first coastal areas to feel the impact of cheap travel facilities were North Wales, Kent and Essex. The last two, in particular, so close to the metropolis with its population of nearly a million, were soon invaded by 'trippers' who steamed down river for the day and by families whose male members worked in London during the week and arrived for the weekend on steamers, popularly known in song and cartoon as the 'Husbands' Boats'.

Pleasure boats were introduced on the Thames in 1815, and soon superseded the Margate hoys which had provided an economical means of reaching the seaside. The steamboats made the journey in eight hours as against the ten or more of boats which depended on the vagaries of wind and tide.

By 1835, over 100,000 visitors a year were descending on Margate. A similar development was taking place from Liverpool and Manchester, down the Ship Canal to the Isle of Man, Blackpool, Southport and North Wales. Ten years later, Thomas Cook ran his first excursion to

Merseyside and North Wales and joined the 20,000 or more passengers who crossed the Mersey from Liverpool to the green and fresh countryside of the Wirral peninsula.

Until the trains displaced them as objects of importance, the steamers' arrival was a major attraction at many resorts. Surtees' Mr Jorrocks vividly described his arrival at Margate in the 1830s: 'It was nearly eight o'clock ere the "Royal Adelaide" touched the point of the far famed Margate jetty, a fact that was announced as well by the usual bump and scuttle to the side to get out first, as by the band striking up "God Save The King", and the mate demanding the tickets of the passengers. . . . Two or three other cargoes of Cockneys having arrived before, the whole place was in a commotion and the beach swarmed with spectators as anxious to watch the last disembarkation as they had been to see the first.' When Mr Jorrocks got to the gate at the end 'the tide of fashion became obstructed by the kissings of husbands and wives, the greetings of fathers and sons, the officiousness of porters, the cries of flymen, the importunities of inn keepers, the cards of bathing women, the salutations of donkey drivers, the programmes of librarians, and the rush and push of the inquisitive, and the waters of the "comers" and "stayers" mingled in one common flood of indescribable confusion.'

Despite their early success, the steamers soon faced a struggle to survive. Enormous competition developed as soon as it became evident that here was a promising new business venture for every town and village along a waterway or seacoast. Then, in the 1840s, came the railways. In spite of all, the steamer services, with their romantic appeal to a seafaring nation, continued to operate all round the coast well into the twentieth century. Competition did lead the steamer companies to improve their vessels, increasing their speed and the luxuriousness of their fittings in order to compete with the economy and reliability of train travel.

In 1845, there were twenty-eight steamers plying between London and Gravesend, another twenty-eight on the run from Greenwich to Woolwich, and ten between London and the coastal resorts. By the 1870s the steamer

companies had been obliged to replace their boats with speedier models. In the 1890s the famous Belle Steamers came in on the Thames to extend the services to the coastal towns of Essex and Suffolk, and the Palace Steamers arrived in 1892. In 1900 steam turbines replaced

VIEW OF BRIGHTON FROM ROSE HILL NORTH

THE BRIGHTON RAILROAD

QUADRILLES,

AND

Pavilion Waltz,

Composed for the Pianoforte,

& DEDICATED TO THE

VISITORS OF BRIGHTON,

BY

FRED.K WRIGHT.

Ent. Sta. Hall.   Pr. 4/-

Published by

WRIGHT & SONS,

MUSIC SELLERS TO THE QUEEN & MUSICAL INSTRUMENT DEALERS,

ROYAL COLONADE, BRIGHTON

the old engines but by this time passengers were being lost in alarming numbers to the railways. Long before the First World War had put an end to the great days of the steamers, the railways had become the most popular way of getting to the seaside.

Brighton was the first major seaside town to feel the effects of the railway, the line arriving there in 1841. Despite opposition from some residents, who demonstrated against the railway on the day of its inauguration, it soon helped Brighton to become Britain's most popular resort. In the first six months of 1844, the Brighton railway carried 360,000 passengers.

Blackpool, Southport and Scarborough were all linked to the railway system by the mid-1840s, and for them all it meant a sudden increase in size and prosperity.

Scarborough's railway arrived in 1845, despite the opposition of people like the author of an anti-railway broadside who wrote that 'the watering place had no wish for a greater influx of vagrants and those who have no money to spend', and who also doubted the railway's ability to make money, even by carrying fish which 'would not amount to £300 per annum'.

How wrong the writer was! Only three years later, the railway was taking so many people to Scarborough that at least one visitor was not pleased. 'This place was very full for there were 4 Special Trains from various parts on the same day a most foolish thing,' wrote the visitor in his diary on 14 August 1848. 'The Railway brought in at the least 3,500 people to the Town.' Going home was not well done either: 'Went in a fly to the station where the scene baffles all attempts at description–the confusion was altogether unnecessary but there was no attempt at forethought on the part of the Railway officials–Mary and Emma tumbled down in the rush and scramble and Mary hurt herself a good deal–We went and returned in 2nd class carriage. . . . Upon the whole the journey was very well performed and clear of any accident–and all I think were well satisfied. The train must have paid the Railway Company well.–If I should ever travel by a Special Train I will learn to go *at the time named for starting* not before–the crushing is over and you are certain to be in time.'

The second class compartments on scheduled trains, which were seldom crowded, were to become the province of the middle classes. The third class carriages and the crowded excursion trains were left to the working classes and day trippers, and the first class carriages to the rich. And the rich could travel in style indeed.

Ellen Buxton, a young member of the famous Quaker family, described in her diary a journey to Cromer in 1864. The family carriage, two carriage horses, five ponies and Papa's riding horse were all put on the train, and the family occupied a splendid saloon carriage. 'It certainly was most comfortable and *beautifully* fitted up. There was a table in the middle, two easy chairs, a sofa fixed to the wall at one side. There was also a little carriage opening out of this big one, which we called the nursery, and there was a wash basin and a place for the luggage,' wrote Ellen.

The extension of the railway network to resort areas was restricted by the high cost of building over difficult terrain, and by the low revenue which could be expected from resorts with little scope for development. Thus, many places in Dorset, Devon, Cornwall and Wales were without a railway for many years and consequently remained small. Others, including several resorts which are still big today, were dependent on the extension of an existing line. Bournemouth, whose railway had to be built to it from the line at Poole, did not get its first trains until 1870.

On the whole, however, by the turn of the century, the coastal resorts of Britain were well served by railways, and wherever the railway reached the resident population was increased as tradesmen, pedlars, entertainers and people in all kinds of professions set up to cater for the visitors.

Among the most noticeable, because their work kept them out in the streets, were the people who provided the transport in the resorts. The first the visitor would notice would be the flymen at the station entrance, who were often paid by local landladies to drive custom in their direction, and whose vehicles were usually very worn-out victorias and landaus. Then there would be the dogcarts and goat-carts waiting for custom along the promenades and around the pier entrances; the string of donkeys, which usually did their work on the sand but which were sometimes used on the streets as well; and even–in Scarborough anyway–jockey carriages whose sad-looking ponies and donkeys were driven by boys in jockeys' caps and breeches.

Trams became part of the seaside scene at quite an early stage in the development of resorts. They were particularly welcome on the piers, where they answered the problem of how to get luggage-laden passengers to and from the steamers as quickly and neatly as possible. Horse tramways were operating on the first Southend Pier in 1845 and along Ryde Pier in 1864.

The first Act of Parliament for a street tramway granted the Landport and Southsea Company in 1863 the right to run a line between Portsmouth Town station and Clarence Pier. The line was opened in 1865 and was horse-drawn.

Electrification first came to Britain's passenger railways at the seaside: Magnus Volk's amazing Electric Railway began operating along the seafront at Brighton from the Palace Pier to Black Rock in 1883. The line was later extended to Kemp Town and then, in the 1890s, to Rottingdean, where part of its journey had to be along the

A familiar sight for thousands of holidaymakers: Brighton railway station at the turn of the century.

23

The Excursion Train Galop (1862) by Frank Musgrave, who specialised in travel and holiday songs, celebrates the excitement of the excursion train and particularly its crowded third-class carriages.

THE EXCURSION TRAIN GALOP

THIRD - CLASS

S. E. R.

BY

FRANK MUSGRAVE.

LONDON BOOSEY & SONS 24 & 28 HOLLES STREET.

shore-line. At high tide the track was submerged, so Volk raised his carriages on stilt-like legs. Soon his train had been dubbed the 'Daddy-long-legs'.

To Blackpool went the honour of having the first electric street tramway in England, opened in 1885. In a few years electrification had come to most pier and street tramways and by the turn of the century even Walton-on-the-Naze's wooden pier had an electric tramway running down its length. By this time, of course, the development of the internal combustion engine had brought the omnibus on the scene. Milnes Daimler omnibuses appeared in Eastbourne in 1903, and the first London to Brighton omnibus made the trip in August 1905.

Throughout the Edwardian summers the vehicles of several generations—landaus and donkey-carts, automobiles and bicycles, trams and char-à-bancs—were to jostle together along the seafronts and promenades, adding colour and variety to the seaside scene.

Left
A page of advertisements from Cook's publication, the *Excursionist and Tourist Advertiser*. Thomas Cook arranged his own special excursion trains all over Britain, particularly to seaside resorts, and also sold the tickets of a number of railway companies.

Below
The Mumbles-Oystermouth Railway was the first passenger railway in Britain and began operating in 1807 with horse-drawn cars. Later, steam engines drew the train's open carriages.

Landing at Clovelly.

Above
There was no pier for the paddle steamers visiting Clovelly, and visitors were ferried ashore in rowing boats.
Centre
The entrance to the railway station at Scarborough in 1913. The building in the background is the Pavilion Hotel.
Below
Visitors to Ramsgate found that the train deposited them right at the edge of the sands.

Ramsgate Sands.

The Station, Scarborough.

Above
A pleasure boat passing the harbour lighthouse at Ramsgate. This attractive scene was often reproduced on pictorial souvenir china of the late nineteenth century.
Below
The steamer 'Duchess of Devonshire', having disembarked her passengers straight on to the beach, manoeuvres her way out of Oddicombe Beach, near Torquay.

...shire leaving Oddicombe Beach, Torquay.

Pier Pavilion, Bognor

24 BOURNEMOUTH. — On the Pier. — LL.

Above, top
Steamers ran to a fairly tight schedule between
resorts. These late arrivals are having to rush down
Bognor Pier to be in time for the already crowded
steamer moored at the pavilion.

Above
The 'Balmoral' from Southampton tied up at
Bournemouth Pier, *c.* 1912.

Above, top
The 'Yarmouth Belle' arriving at Clacton-on-Sea in
1914. The Belle Steamers were owned by the Coast
Development Company, who also owned piers at
several resorts round the Thames Estuary.

Above
Boarding 'La Marguerite' at Llandudno Pier.
During the summer there were always big crowds
at the steamer landing stages.

Right
A promenade bathchair with a full complement, *c.* 1898. Will there be room for the dog?
Below
Goat-carts, usually driven by boys, were a popular means of transport in many resorts. This scene was photographed at the end of Edward VII's reign.

Left
Magnus Volk's Electric Overland and Submarine Railway, nick-named 'Daddy long-legs' was a familiar sight in Brighton at the end of the century. When it began running along the sea front in 1883 it was the first electric railway in Britain. In 1896 Volk extended it along the beach and, therefore, into the sea, to Rottingdean. This section stopped running in 1900.

Below
No seaside holiday was complete without a donkey ride.

Seaside Donkeys.

Above
Cliff railways and lifts (or funiculars, as they are called in Europe) were a familiar feature at many British resorts. The first to be built in England was the South Cliff tramway at Scarborough. It was opened in 1875 and linked the Esplanade with the Spa.

Facing page, top
An open-top tram on the South Promenade at Blackpool, where the first electric street tramway system in England was opened in 1885.

Facing page, centre and bottom
'Love to Mother from Blackpool' in 1908 came with this picture of a 'Dreadnought' tram at the Gynn Inn terminus of the Blackpool tramway system.

SOUTH PROMENADE, BLACKPOOL.

Gynn Inn, Blackpool.

LOVE TO MOTHER FROM BLACKPOOL

GYNN INN

1ᵈ POST CARD

VICTORIA SERIES.

Published by E. R. G. & Co., Blackpool

No. 64

THIS SPACE CAN BE USED FOR CORRESPONDENCE.

THE ADDRESS ONLY TO BE WRITTEN HERE.

Dear Mother,
Have had no time to write before, have seen Bessie, but not Alfred, am having the time of my life, wish I was stopping a month. Sarah. XXXX

Mrs H Miles
32 Sackville St
Todmorden

MARINE PARADE, GREAT YARMOUTH.

LONDON MOTOR OMNIBUS COMPANY LIMITED
VANGUARD

The Char-a-bancs, Bridlington

Facing page, top
Both horse-drawn and electric
trams feature in this picture of
Marine Parade, Great Yarmouth.

Facing page, bottom
The first London to Brighton motor
omnibus starting out on its journey,
30 August, 1905.

Above
The old and the new at Bridlington:
a solid-tyred motorised char-a-banc
and a horse-drawn one ready to
start out on an excursion.

Well-ordered Watering Places

IN 1850 the seaside resort was still in its infancy. Of those which later became famous only Brighton, Ramsgate, Margate, Scarborough, Weymouth, Torquay, Dover, Ilfracombe, Ryde, Cowes and Worthing were of any importance. Blackpool, with a population of a mere 2,180, Eastbourne with only 3,433 and Bournemouth with 695 residents hardly rated as resorts at all.

The development of a resort was largely a matter of luck in the topography of its situation: places like Brighton or Southend, approached by a broad valley or by a flat hinterland, encouraged railway builders to extend lines in their direction. If they happened to be near a large city their clientele was assured. So was the interest of land developers who were constantly on the alert for the business opportunities presented by the new facility of movement and ease of communication given by the railways. In the second half of the century the combined interests of the railways and land developers and the snowballing enthusiasm for travel felt by an ever-growing number of Britain's 18 million inhabitants increased the pace of seaside development.

Often the development of seaside estates was the work of one or two individuals: Eastbourne, for example, was the creation of the Dukes of Devonshire; Torquay grew thanks to the enthusiasm of Sir Lawrence Palk; Bournemouth was developed by Sir George William Tapps and Decimus Burton. Not all such ventures were fortunate: Sir Richard Hotham who tried to establish Bognor as a seaside resort was before his time and at Ravenscar, north of Scarborough, the resort hardly got beyond its foundations.

As the seaside resorts multiplied, so the competition

between them increased and more and more investment was made in amenities that would attract the visitor and his money. More often than not the cost of building and maintaining the attractions proved to be greater than the revenue they produced. As well as competition between resorts, there was rivalry among businessmen within a town who hoped to reap a profit from the visitors and this produced business failures as well as successes. In Blackpool, the competition between the Tower company and the one which ran the Winter Garden led to the latter building a giant wheel in an attempt to rival the Tower itself: the wheel was never profitable and was eventually dismantled.

The first amenities built with visitors in mind were of a more fundamental character, providing elementary services, which are now taken for granted but which in the mid-nineteenth century were a major attraction. One of the first and most popular of these amenities was the promenade or parade. Starting as a stretch of earth between the houses and the highest point of the tide this frontier between the town and the sea became the most frequented part of the resort. After a stone wall was built to strengthen the earthen barrier a road and pavement was laid along its length and on this the visitor promenaded much as they had done in former times along the crescents of Bath or the Pantiles of Tunbridge Wells. Sometimes, as in Broadstairs, Southport and Scarborough, the promenade extended up the slopes and valleys of the cliffs through gardens and wooded glades.

Until the piers were developed as an extension of the promenades into the sea, the parades and marinas were as close as the visitor could get to the ocean. Their design was a constant reminder of the proximity to Neptune's kingdom, with railings which echoed those found on board ships, bollards shaped like capstans, and lamp standards and other products of the iron foundry decorated with mermaids, sea serpents, anchors and other objects associated with the sea.

Since seaside resorts were developed by private capital at a time when the idiosyncratic Victorian sense of identity was at its strongest it was inevitable that the orderly design which had characterised the Regency

period should be completely swamped by a variety of ill-assorted styles. To the unbiased modern eye conditioned to dull uniformity, the undisciplined ferment of Victorian seaside architecture is in keeping with the sense of freedom associated with holidays. At any rate, the architects and builders of the new resorts felt no nostalgia for the neat façades of the Regency terraces. (Bexhill, created by the Earl de la Warr, who hoped to set the tone suitable for an upper-class resort with his Palladian façades, was a rare exception.) Instead they went wild with medieval castles and evocations of Venetian palaces, Tudor mansions, and oriental pavilions. Brighton had set the style for the latter and the domes and fretted arches, ogival windows and slender pillars of the Regent's Pavilion were echoed in the buildings of many seaside resorts.

Many of the characteristics of seaside architecture were dictated by the ethos of the seaside: the yearning to gaze on the sea was satisfied by the provision of houses with balconies and bay windows 'with a sea view' (the old

Bexhill was a late-comer to the seaside scene, and when this photograph was taken around 1895, the resort was still developing under the auspices of Earl de la Warr, the chief landowner. It was just a fishing village until it added the words 'on-Sea' to its name in 1884, thus announcing its intention of joining the seaside resort race.

fishing villages were built with their backs to the sea as protection from winter gales); the search for the health-giving properties of sea water was answered by vast and rather ponderous hydropathic establishments; and the need to show off to one's neighbours, vital to the self-esteem of the newly-risen middle class, was provided for by the Grand Hotels which gave prestige to those resorts which had the most luxuriously appointed ones.

Another class of building which saw a great boom by the sea was the religious. Churches sprang up like mushrooms in Medieval, Renaissance, Egyptian, Greek and other more homely styles to accommodate the different sects whose members arrived at the seaside resorts. In Scarborough, the town guide boasted that 'probably no other town in the Empire of the same size, possesses a greater number of places of worship of God than Scarborough'.

A quite different architectural feature of seaside resorts was the Winter Garden. This was a building with a cast-iron structure covered with glass like a huge greenhouse.

The front at Hastings in the 1890s. Earlier in the century, Hastings had been popular with aristocratic visitors. Lord Byron and Louis Napoleon stayed there and King Louis Philippe of France spent part of his exile at the Victoria Hotel in 1848. Charles Lamb described his stay there as 'a dreary penance'.

No doubt inspired by the Crystal Palace of the 1851 Exhibition, the Winter Garden provided a delightful meeting place where visitors to the seaside could listen to music, take tea, or just stroll about among the palms and ferns which gave the illusion of being in those warmer climes to which the better off went in winter time.

Since social curiosity was a powerful motivation in the daily life of visitors, most resorts provided as many gathering places as they could afford. Among the most attractive were the public gardens, most of them laid out with tree-lined walks, ornamental ponds, rustic bridges, garden seats and a bandstand where bands of all kinds, but mostly military, played to rows of attentive listeners who had paid a modest sum for a chair in the area round the stand.

The place of the bandstand as the centrepiece of the garden made its design a matter of importance and here, as in other architectural features of resorts, there is evidence of the designers' attempts to outdo the bandstands of rival resorts. Many resorts had two or three bandstands and styles ranged from fairly functional circular platforms with a roof to miniature copies of the Brighton Pavilion.

In time, more mundane features such as sanitation and public services became as important assets to a resort as bandstands and Winter Gardens. Good sanitation, in particular, became essential as people grew more conscious of hygiene. Often, battles raged in the press about the pollution or lack of it at leading watering places and many cartoons commented wryly on the 'ozone' at the seaside. The main problem was that of sewage disposal. In the early days, with only small numbers of visitors, resorts dealt with sewage either by the cesspool method or simply by allowing it to flow into the sea. As more and more people went seabathing this became impossible. In the watchful columns of the local newspapers, many of which existed largely for the summer visitor, defects in the sewage disposal system were immediately pointed out.

On the other hand, any resort which had installed a sewage system was quick to announce it. A guide to Thanet published in 1890 drew attention to the improvements in the sewage system of Margate: 'The town is abundantly well supplied with excellent water from the pure wells of the chalk formation. Its sanitary arrangements are most satisfactory, an entirely new system being just completed, at the cost of about £75,000. The whole drainage of the town is conducted to an outfall on the east and two miles distant from the town whence it is discharged into the sea at a distance of 250 yards beyond high water mark and into the Channel which carries it right away towards the German Ocean and the North Pole.'

In their rivalry the resorts were not averse to denigrating each other. The east coast resorts compared their own calm seas with those along other coasts: 'the continual swell and surf of the sea on the south coast of England, which not only makes the water there foul and thick but annoys, frightens, and spatters the bathers exceedingly.'

By the turn of the century many resorts had become large towns with every urban amenity including electric light, well-paved streets, local transport facilities and a local council which energetically did everything in its

Although joined to Hastings by a line of terraces and parades, St Leonards maintained a more select atmosphere and its stately buildings were in keeping with its clientele.

power to attract more revenue-bearing visitors.

In the early twentieth century there were nearly 300 established resorts in the British Isles and their population doubled and trebled during the summer months. Most of them had developed individual characteristics which had grown out of the nature of their visitors. The Lancashire coastal resorts were typical of the divergence of life styles. Blackpool, which catered for the working class from the industrial towns inland, was big, boisterous and noisy while Southport maintained a more reserved

The Mumbles, in South Wales, was close enough to Swansea to count as the city's seaside suburb.

atmosphere suitable for families and older people. Lytham St Anne's was even more withdrawn and its rich residents hidden behind their hedges and walls kept themselves to themselves and did not encourage the development of promenades or other areas that attracted crowds. All round the coasts the same class divisions were discernible with resorts like Eastbourne, Bexhill, Torquay and Frinton fighting to preserve themselves from the trippers who arrived in their thousands at Southend, Margate, Llandudno, Brighton, Clacton, Weston-super-Mare and others.

Seaside resorts had become an industry by the Edwardian period and vast sums of money were spent in developing the facilities of existing resorts and building new ones.

Life at the resorts became more regulated and the experimental styles of the early years became the traditions of the new communities by the sea which, while they reflected some of the aspects of the cities from which the visitors came, somehow transformed them into more bizarre and imaginative shape.

On the beach at Great Yarmouth, the class distinctions of Victorian life faded away in the jovial atmosphere which characterised the town. In the background of this picture two of Great Yarmouth's three piers are visible.

SCARBOROUGH, FROM THE SPA GROUNDS.

Above
A general view of Scarborough, *c.* 1905, with the Spa grounds in the foreground. The Spa Saloon, opened in 1880, housed the mineral springs which had brought Scarborough to the attention of health seekers in the eighteenth century.

Facing page, top
Aldeburgh in the mid-1890s. This small resort, described by Wilkie Collins as 'a curious little outpost on the shores of England', lacked the good sands which might have made it a more popular resort.

Facing page, bottom
Ventnor, Isle of Wight, owed much of its success as a seaside resort to having been mentioned in Sir James Clark's *The Influence of Climate in the Prevention and Cure of Diseases*. In 1895, the author of *Round the Coast* wrote that 'Ventnor is essentially a place that has been made by doctors, and nothing can be more astonishing than the rapidity with which the tiny fishing hamlet has been transformed into a fashionable resort'.

PIERROTS AT THE NEW SPA, BRIDLINGTON.

Went on here last night but was just too late to hear the Pierrots. B. S.

Above
The New Spa at Bridlington had the air of a conservatory.
Left
The delicately-scented pine trees which were a feature of Bournemouth were said to be one of the reasons for the wonderfully healthy atmosphere of this most genteel of resorts. Here, the trees line the rather depressingly-named Invalids' Walk.
Below
The Prince Regent ensured the future prosperity of Brighton when, as Prince of Wales, he began spending much of his time there. His notorious Pavilion gave the town some of the most original seaside architecture ever devised, and set a fashion for exotic styles.

INVALIDS' WALK, BOURNEMOUTH

...ilion, Brighton

Above
Wrought-iron work was a major
feature of seaside architecture and
its design was often elaborate,
including such motifs as fish,
mermaids, dolphins and anchors.
The entrance to the New Spa
Gardens at Bridlington was
decorated with fine scroll work.
Right
The Indian Lounge in the Winter
Gardens, Blackpool. 'Entertainment
All Day and Not a Dull Moment'
was the slogan painted at the
entrance (admission sixpence) to the
famous Winter Gardens.
Below
The Floral Hall, Brighton

47

The Fish Market, Brighton.

Above
The Fish Market, Brighton, was a popular early-
morning scene with visitors and frugal landladies
alike.
Below
Scarborough was famous for the beauty of her
formal gardens, most of which were laid out
between 1887 and 1914. This is the Italian Terrace,
next to the Spa.

ITALIAN TERRACE THE SPA SCARBOROUGH

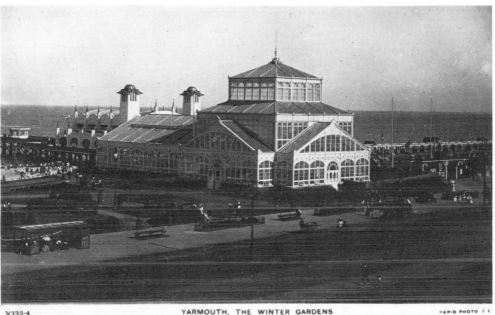

V332-4 YARMOUTH, THE WINTER GARDENS. RAPID PHOTO £ C

Above
Great Yarmouth's Winter Gardens looked like a
giant greenhouse, and gave its visitors the
impression of summer all the year round.
Below
One of the principal amusements at the seaside
resort was the band concert, and most bandstands
were very ornate in style. This bandstand at
Southend had glass panels which could be moved
round to protect the bandsmen from the wind.

THE BAND STAND, SOUTHEND-ON-SEA.

Above
Despite its grand name, the Royal
Parade at Eastbourne was a simple
promenade running between the
road and the sea.

Right
The promenade at Aberystwyth in
the 1890s was a fairly primitive
affair, compared with those of larger
resorts.

Below
The Great Orme provides a splendid back drop for
an open-air concert in the Happy Valley at
Llandudno.

52

The Pavilion, Weymouth.

PAVILION TORQUAY

Above, top
The Pavilion at Weymouth, displaying almost as
many domes as St Basil's Cathedral in Moscow.

Above
This picture of the Pavilion at Torquay has an
imperial air, with the Union Jacks floating over the
bandstands and the entrance.

All the Comforts of Home

In the early days of the seaside holiday, resorts were often no more than a cluster of villas set behind a fishing village, or built on hillsides and in valleys by developers whose estates were designed to attract the upper classes wishing to spend winter weeks in the health-giving vicinity of the sea.

With the arrival of the railways, these selected communities with their backs to the sea grew into villages and towns and acquired all the features of full-blown resorts. In time, the largest of them would acquire the great hotels with the splendid names—Imperial, Metropole, Royal, Britannia, Great Eastern—which were the prototypes of all the Grand Hotels of Edwardian Europe.

But at the beginning of the Victorian period, what accommodation there was left a lot to be desired. More often than not, the visitor, having fought off the importunities of the many eager cab drivers who vied for custom at the exits of most seaside railway stations, would arrive at some unprepossessing house, the most noticeable feature of which would be the heavy smell of mutton chops and cabbage.

Most lodgings were in private houses, in smarter terraces for more genteel visitors, and in small backstreet cottages which had once belonged to local fishermen, for working-class visitors. They were run by landladies who provided no food but were prepared to cook, and filch, the foods provided by their tenants.

Robert Horatio Green, writing about Brighton in 1862, categorised landladies as either vultures or crocodiles:

'The first,' he wrote, 'is generally at the top of the kitchen staircase, ready to pounce upon the newcomer, while the latter usually ensconces herself behind the flowerpots in the parlour, gazing with hungry looks at the passers-by like an alligator in the sedges. The vulture preys upon you openly and at once. She feeds her helps out of your larder and she makes the tradesmen give her a percentage for her recommendation. She attempts to make you pay for her butcher's bill and when you cut up rough, she assumes the air of injured innocence and shadows forth an action for defamation at the next assizes. . . .'

The crocodile is more subtle: 'She hopes you will never suspect her of taking advantage, and, till the weekly bill is presented you really believe you have found a true female Samaritan to pour oil into your wounds. This upon experience you find that she certainly could do, only she would irritate your wounds and overcharge you for the oil.'

Lodging houses were particularly in demand by families, as the few hotels in existence were not inclined to accept children. The alternatives to lodging houses were houses where food was provided at communal tables. Dr Granville, whose records of journeys round the resorts of Britain entitle him to claim to be the first professional travel journalist, described one of these establishments: 'We were admitted into a long and lofty apartment having some pretensions to the rank of a banqueting room, in which a long narrow table, groaning under a double line of tin capped dishes, was awaiting the arrival of the company. A long sounding, scavenger-like bell soon brought the latter, mob-fashion into the room. . . . Such a motley of honest-looking people, men, women and children (for there were some whose chins did not reach the edge of the table) it has never been my fortune to meet under like circumstances in such numbers before, fifty or sixty in all. Highest in rank here might have been an iron founder from near Halifax, or a retired merchant from Liverpool.'

One feels that conditions could not have been as bad as they were described by writer after writer, from the great Dickens and Thackeray to the unknown compilers of anonymous guide books, for after all, people kept going back to the seaside. But there were plenty of complaints,

most of them along similar lines: the people were dreadful, the landladies were dishonest and the food, when it was provided, was atrocious.

'I take two spoonfuls of soup and find that it resembles a mixture of warm table beer, thoroughly peppered . . .' wrote Green, describing his first meal. The main course was not much to his liking either: 'a piece of mutton, streaking my plate with carmine, is now at my disposal; but as I deem that eating raw mutton is simply eating raw sheep without the benefit of the wool to comfort your insides I cast about to see whether an entree of some sort is an impossibility. . . . I helped myself to a dish before me but to this day I am not certain of its composition. It was full of knots and kernels of such toughness, that if you were not careful and kept close watch in regard to the proprieties, they would spring out of your mouth in a

The hotels of the early period of the seaside holiday were frequently converted private houses, and often stood alone by a beach or sheltered cove. This picture from an 1840s' guide to the Isle of Wight shows Plumbly's Hotel, Freshwater Bay.

PLUMBLY'S HOTEL,
FRESHWATER BAY, ISLE OF WIGHT.

manner entirely subversive to the decencies of the dining table. . . . I am forced to the conclusion that it is neither more nor less than stewed india rubber.'

If the food was often inedible, it was also served in a slovenly way, or else was dreadfully slow in coming. Two

American ladies, describing their bicycle tour of England and Wales in 1881 complained of it at the George in Portsmouth; Sir Leslie Stephen, writing in the CORNHILL MAGAZINE in 1869, had gone further and said quite categorically, 'That the lodging house is a torment, has become notorious . . . with a slatternly landlady downstairs, and a select party of parasitical insects in the bedrooms, in which the English paterfamilias consumes uneatable food.'

The 'parasitical insects' were a notorious hazard of seaside life, even occasionally in the more genteel terraces and large hotels, and featured in many cartoons in periodicals like PUNCH as well as in story and song.

The prevalence of bugs is borne out by the numerous advertisements for Keatings powder in the local newspapers, and by the following ditty, which is an item of seaside folklore:

'I am a bug, a seaside bug,
When folks in bed are lying snug,
About their skin we walk and creep,
And feast upon them while they sleep,
In lodging houses, where we breed
And at this season largely feed.'

While the working classes struggled with bugs and rapacious landladies and middle-class families made do with poor food and indifferent sanitation, the wealthy entered into a period of ostentatious comfort at the seaside. The 1860s saw the beginning of a rapid growth in hotel building to cater for the well-off. This was the period of such monumental architectural piles as the Grand at Brighton and the Great Eastern in Harwich, both opened in 1864, the Grand at Scarborough, opened with splendid ceremony in 1867, and the Metropole at Blackpool.

Among the greatest of the early hotels, and one which set the style for those that came later was the Grand Hotel at Scarborough, built in the Italian style with a wealth of architectural detail, and which still stands today, a venue for political party conferences.

The Grand had the advantage of one of the most commanding sites of any resort in Britain. On the cliff above Scarborough's South Bay it towers over the resort as castles and cathedrals once did over medieval villages.

Like many hotels of its period, the Grand sought to provide for a high-class winter clientele as well as the parties made up of families and successful industrialists who arrived in the summer months. For the winter visitor the Grand provided heating with Haden's Warming Apparatus, and a conservatory to give him the illusion that he was in the South of France.

Three years earlier Brighton had opened its own Grand Hotel, described by the BRIGHTON HERALD as standing on 'our cliffs like Saul amidst the men of Israel'. Like the Grand at Scarborough, it had many Italian features including tiled walls, balconies and Florentine windows and doorways. In an age when all invention was a symbol of progress the Grand at Brighton had much to be proud of: there were completely self-contained catering facilities including a bakehouse, fish and roasting kitchens, a confectionery, wine and beer cellars and an ice-house. Listed among its equipment were 12 miles of bell wire, 230 marble chimney pieces and five passenger lifts which operated by means of 'down pressure of a 60 ft column of water being so applied as to drive the ram which upheaves the platform'.

Hotel building flourished in the decades after 1860 and the variety of hotels increased.

Winter was a time when the upper classes, following the example of Lord Brougham, increasingly were leaving the shores of Britain for those of the Riviera and the hotels, therefore, had to work hard to persuade their patrons that a winter holiday at Scarborough, Torquay, Brighton, Southport or Ramsgate was every bit as good as one taken at Cannes.

The Granville Hotel at Ramsgate used powerful arguments in its newspaper advertising: 'There can be no doubt that when the remarkable advantages offered to visitors by the Granville are known, it will become one of the most favourite residences in England. Its close contiguity to London—for the iron horse practically annihilates such a trifling distance as eighty odd miles—is one of its recommendations. A week or a fortnight during the murkiest of the months is just the sort of pick-up which a professional man, if he once experienced its inestimable value, would frequently have recourse to.

And for that class of invalid who has not yet made it a matter of religion to winter in Pau, or Nice or Algiers, and who are sensible enough to know that baths of every description can be obtained in England just as easily as in any pokey German town let them, if their desire to be braced up is genuine, try a course of Granvilles.'

By 1900, the small professional hotel catering for 'families and commercial gentlemen' was well established and even the seaside landladies, aware that the tide was turning in favour of their customers, were trying to provide better accommodation. The old practice whereby the landlady cooked and served food provided by the families staying with her was disappearing in favour of 'bed and breakfast' or full board in houses whose dining rooms might boast 'separate tables'.

At Scarborough, Mrs Bailey claimed among other things that her house had perfect sanitation, while Mrs Buckle down the street offered entertainment in the form of a piano and Mrs Purnell went one better with an American organ. Competition, as it usually does, was improving standards and at every level there was accommodation available in resorts which would continue to grow at a great rate throughout the Edwardian age.

The Albion Hotel, Broadstairs, now a Trust Houses Forte Hotel, dates from Regency times, and has not altered much from the days when Dickens stayed a few houses along the road.

KING'S HEAD HOTEL
SANDOWN ISLE OF WIGHT

Coaches to all parts
POSTING

C. Elkins, PROPRIETOR

Wines Spirits Ales &c
of the best quality

Above
The King's Head Hotel
at Sandown in the
1840s.
Right
Rising in solitary
splendour over the
sandhills, the hotel at
Aberavon at the turn of
the century.

Aberavon.

L.T. SILLETT
STAR & GARTER HOTEL
Upper Sandown, Isle of Wight
Coaches to all parts   Posting in all its branches
CHOICE WINES SPIRITS &c &c

The Beach and Hotel.

Above
A Brighton boarding-house dinner, illustrated in an 1862 book about the town. Landladies who provided food at their houses were not renowned for their culinary skill, and meals were more often suffered than enjoyed.

Below
The horrors of boarding-house life were the subject of many seaside postcards. In this one, American tinned meat is the butt of the simple humour traditional to the genre.

PATERFAMILIAS HAS HIS HOLIDAY AT THE SEA-SIDE—

Above
The family at their seaside lodgings.
A cartoon by John Leech, published
in *Punch* in 1857.

Below
If the stories are to be believed,
seaside visitors had to put up with
whatever sleeping arrangements
they could get.

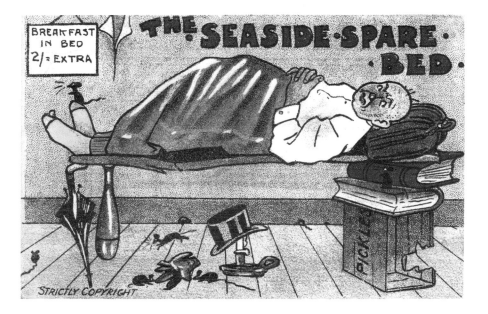

FULL UP

Left
A postcard summing up the fate of
many visitors to the seaside.
Bathing cabins or boats drawn up
on the beach, often served as
temporary sleeping accommodation.
Below, left
The bedbug was a part of seaside
mythology throughout the
Victorian and Edwardian period.
Facing page
It was the custom for boarding-
house parties to have their holidays
immortalized by the camera. These
parties were photographed at
Cliftonville, Margate and at
Lowestoft.

LYNDALE. EDGAR RD. CLIFTONVILLE. MARGATE.

Facing page, top
Despite the make-shift appearance
of the roof girders and supports, the
Lounge and Buffet of the Palace by
the Sea, Clacton, with its stiff table
linen and potted palms, manages to
suggest a certain grandeur.

Facing page, bottom
Those people who lived in rooms or
had booked a hotel on a bed and
breakfast basis, had to find
somewhere to have their meals. In
Brighton, a favourite place was
Muttons, which was a hotel as well
as a restaurant.

Left
Inside Muttons in the 1860s. Here,
one could drink soup, eat pies, sip a
glass of wine or port, and meet one's
friends.

Below
One of the first of the great hotels
was at Scarborough. Dominating the
St Nicholas Cliff, the Grand Hotel
was designed by Cuthbert Broderick
in the Italian style and opened in
1867.

Below
Brighton remained the Queen of resorts, and her
hotels, including the Grand and Metropole shown
here, acquired a reputation for smartness and later
a risqué character because of their patronage by
the London smart set.
Bottom
Many hotels grew great from small beginnings. One
such was the Metropole at Blackpool which began
life as the much smaller Bailey's hotel in the
eighteenth century. It was extended in 1876, as this
illustration from the re-building prospectus shows.

Brighton   Hôtel Metropole and the Grand Hôtel

With kisses from father

A Dip in the Briny

As more and more people came to spend their holidays at the seaside, bathing ceased to be just a medical ritual carried out under doctors' instructions, and became part of the fun of a seaside holiday.

Even so, it was a long time before the seabathing part of the holiday became an informal jaunt from the beach out into the water. Victoria's reign was well over before respectable women could be seen strolling about the beach in their swimming costumes. Even the day trippers paddling about at the water's edge, whooping and shrieking and jumping about for the joy of it, rather than wasting time and money queueing up for a bathing machine to swim from, did not undress and go swimming from the beach until Edwardian times.

For decades, the bathing machines and their notorious attendants ruled the visitors' sea.

Scarborough and Margate vie for the honour of having been the first seaside watering place to introduce the bathing machine in England. The winner would appear to have been Scarborough: a print of Scarborough in 1736, made from an engraving by John Setterington, clearly shows a wheeled hut drawn up at the water's edge, its naked occupant about to step into the sea. It was not until the 1750s that Margate's famous Benjamin Beale introduced his machines with the modesty hoods, which ladies could shelter under as they stepped from the machine into the water.

By the early nineteenth century most resorts had a collection of bathing machines for visitors' use. This room on wheels, which cost sixpence or one shilling to hire, including towels, was dragged out into the water by a horse and provided the privacy of the indoor bathing establishment, in theory at least, and no lady would have considered bathing without its protective presence.

In the bigger resorts, men used them too. There were always more bathers than there were machines, and many resorts provided waiting rooms in which people waiting for machines to become free, could read newspapers, drink tea or coffee and even play on a piano, all provided by the proprietors of the rooms.

Unless one was lucky enough to get it early in the day, the machine was a very unattractive object: damp, ill-lit, ill-ventilated, its floor covered with sand and the seawater which had dripped from its previous occupants and perhaps even sloshed up the steps of the machine while it was out in the sea, it was also set in motion as soon as its hirer was inside. He or she had to change into their bathing costume as best they could in such a confined space while the machine jolted and shook its way down the beach and into the water.

For men, the bathing machine had few attractions. It was cumbersome, unnecessary and did not compare with the joy of rushing into the sea naked in the way that men always had. By the 1850s, this masculine freedom was being eroded and men were only allowed to bathe on certain parts of the beach and at certain times, indicated by the ringing of a bell. Also, more conformist or less freedom-loving people were criticising the behaviour of those who enjoyed their bathe in the traditional manner. Some, like a writer to the SCARBOROUGH GAZETTE in 1851, helpfully tried to find a compromise: 'If the correspondent in your last week's paper signed "A Visitor" had, when at Brighton, extended his visit to Hastings he would have seen there in practice a very simple remedy for the evils of which he complains; no gentleman there is allowed to bathe without a pair of drawers.'

The male habit of bathing nude took a long time to die, all the same. There was another complaint to the SCARBOROUGH GAZETTE in 1866 that 'At Scarborough hundreds of men and women may be seen in the water – the men stark naked and the women so loosely and insufficiently clad that for all purposes of decency they might as well have been naked too.'

On the whole, men did not want to bathe with the

women and the French habit of mixed bathing which had been introduced at the unlikely resort of Llandudno was not generally approved. One indignant correspondent of the SCARBOROUGH GAZETTE who signed himself 'A Bather' wrote, 'We have most of us heard of this French style of bathing; but Englishmen be it remembered are not Frenchmen, and when they go to bathe they go in order that they may enjoy, as unencumbered as possible, a manly and health-giving exercise. As for dancing the quadrilles and such like pastimes, which the French indulge in in the water, surely these may be deferred to other and more fitting opportunities.'

In 1874, the Rev. Francis Kilvert could still write in his diary, 'At Shanklin one has to adopt the detestable custom of bathing in drawers. If ladies don't like to see men naked why don't they keep away from the sight.'

The first bathers who ventured into the sea for pleasure were aided by bathing women, like the famous Martha Gunn at Brighton. In this etching, depicting a variation of a familiar theme, Brighton's Chain Pier is seen in the background.

Published by W.H.Mason, at his Repository of Arts 81 Kings Road, Brighton.

THE FIRST DIP.

Brave words, but he was fighting against the moral tide, and soon the wearing of drawers or calecons, as they were euphemistically called, became obligatory. Eventually the calecon became a costume that covered the whole torso.

The steady increase in the bathing population as more and more people from all classes of society arrived at the seaside helped to perpetuate the attitudes to seabathing as newcomers, eager to do the right thing, adopted the seabathing customs of the regular visitors or followed the counsels of busybodies who gave out streams of advice in the columns of the newspapers or in books of instruction. Here are the correct procedures for taking a bathe, as outlined by Dr Alexander of Scarborough in 1880: 'The plan recommended here', he wrote, 'is that the bather having taken such exercise as is adequate to produce general warmth, should select a dry machine, to be drawn to a sufficient depth into the water to enable him, leisurely descending the steps, to crouch down so as easily to immerse the whole of the body under the water, after which the feeble and debilitated ought immediately to return within the machine and be well rubbed with a close towel, hastily dressing, however, to favour by the warmth of the clothing the conservative glow. He should then gently walk home, avoiding the sun's rays if powerful, or exercise such as would produce perspiration, and on his arrival, if he feel inclined (which sometimes happens) he may partake of a warm bowl of soup, or dish of tea or coffee, as may be preferred, already prepared in the anticipation of the return; but should he experience nausea at the stomach, or a sense of coldness, a little warm sherry wine and water may perhaps be substituted.'

Dr Alexander was less discouraging to those of a robust constitution but he warned that the 'delightful recreation of swimming' could, when carried too far, produce 'the greatest prostration of strength, accompanied with headache, palpitations, quickened respiration, coldness, sickness, tremors, paleness and numbness of extremities and partial loss of circulation.'

In the face of these dire warnings it is a wonder that anyone took to the sea at all, but nothing, it seemed, was more powerful than the urge first to dip oneself in the water and then to master it by learning to float and swim in the unfamiliar element. To do so in company could be better than to do it alone, and soon bathing and swimming clubs began to be formed at the resorts. One of the early ones was at Brighton where in 1858 a group of young men meeting at the Jolly Fisherman Inn joined together to form the Brighton Swimming Club, entrance fee one shilling and twopence per week subscription. The first swimming races took place in 1861 and all competitors were warned that they would not be allowed to compete unless they wore swimming drawers.

Intrepid or careless swimmers were soon to provide those sensational news stories so dear to the readers of the popular press.

'This morning,' said the SCARBOROUGH GAZETTE of 1866, 'was near adding another to the many victims who have been sacrificed at Scarborough owing to the gross and culpable neglect of precautions in case of accidents.' In time, life saving equipment appeared and a system of signals was used to warn of currents and high tides.

Most people did not venture out of the shallow water, and many preferred not to go into the water at all, but to stay on the beach and watch the continuous free show that was presented to them by the musicians, acrobats, pedlars, photographers, fortune tellers, donkey men and ice cream salesmen who vied for the custom of the visitors. A vivid picture of the beach at Yarmouth was painted in an 1877 guide book: 'The central portion of the beach being the most frequented by visitors is also the chief resort, the happy hunting ground of the numerous class who have a keen eye to business. Nearly all are vendors of only one kind of article each, and this peculiarity tends to multiply their numbers, the variety of merchandise among the whole being considerable. There are so many—and some of them strangers to Yarmouth—that were they not civil, and usually take first refusal, persistence with frequency would be an annoyance little short of a nuisance. Take a seat and your troubles begin: "Here's your chocolate creams. Buns two a penny. Yarmouth rock a penny a bar. Apples penny a bag. Hokey Pokey two a penny. Nuts or pears, fine Williams. Lemonade threepence a bottle. Pears or grapes, all ripe, buy a nice bunch of grapes, Sir. Walnuts eight a penny, fine walnuts. Milk, penny a glass." Fancy the effects of such an interruption upon a couple who had passed the spooning period of life and were intently engaged in writing, probably letters to friends, or jotting down their impressions among the sands.'

The crowds that arrived on the beach in summer

became so great that the behaviour of them and of those who worked or resided in the area found itself being regulated by many local laws. Local business interests, with an eye to maintaining the popularity of their resort, began to campaign for the control of beach pedlars and entertainers and for the proper licensing of bathing machines, which at the height of the season were used to sleep in by visitors who had failed to find accommodation. These rules concerned themselves with every aspect of the resort. At Southport, for instance, the Rules and Regulations painted on a board on the beach covered such matters as the distance between the bathing ground appointed for ladies and that for men; the bounds beyond which bathing machines might not be moved; the permissable distance between passing boats and bathing machines (the distance was 30 yards and the fine five shillings); and the disposal of fish offal by local fishermen.

With the gradual disappearance of the bathing machine in Edwardian times, some of the mystery and magic attached to the beach ritual left it. Instead, there was an increasing and rational liberalism; ladies took to bathing from the beach and and even walking about in their

An early photograph of Ramsgate's bathing machines, with their distinctive large canopies. The canopies were supposed to protect bathers from prying eyes, but these ladies do not seem to mind being seen in the water.

bathing costumes. Mixed bathing was allowed at Bexhill in 1901 and other resorts soon followed the lead. The entertainers were enclosed within canvas walls or banished to the pier or town theatre and cafés and shops replaced the itinerant salesmen.

Soon the beach began to lose its character of a fairground where life in all its aspects could be found and became, in most cases, the well-ordered watering place whose respectability and good manners recommended it to its increasingly class-conscious visitors.

Right
Several of the bathing machines photographed here on the beach at Tenby in the mid-1890s carry advertisements for Beecham's Pills—a familiar sight on beaches throughout the country at this time.
Below
Capstans and ropes have replaced horses as the means of getting the bathing machines into the water in this photograph of Ventnor, Isle of Wight.

The Esplanade, Ventnor.

5055   TRAINS DE PLAISIR. — Un Dimanche à la Mer. — LL.

Above, top
This drawing of the Sands at Ramsgate by W.
McConnell gives a lively impression of the crowded
scene on popular beaches in the 1860s.

Above
This photograph by French photographer, 'LL',
much of whose work appeared on British postcards,
hints at why some British people disapproved of
French uninhibited seabathing habits.

The Initiate.

Above, top
The joys of the bucket and spade.
Above
A family group caught by the camera of an itinerant beach photographer.
Facing page, top left
The costume seen here, with knickers peeping coyly out from under a skirt, became popular during the late Victorian period, although the Victorians would never have worn it with the cheerful immodesty of this girl in 1914.

Facing page, top right
An Edwardian pin-up beauty in a costume that probably never went outside the photographer's studio.
Facing page, bottom
In late Edwardian times, the bathing costume became a thin garment of woven cotton which became transparent when wet, and it is little wonder that pictures of bathing beauties lolling by the water's edge became popular.

A Water Nymph.

BEAUTY (PARTLY) UNADORNED.

COULDN'T YOU COME TOO?

Right
Laughter on the steps of a bathing machine, 1912. Judging by the name 'Taylor' on his back, the gentleman has hired his costume.

Below
By the beginning of the twentieth century, the bathing cabin was disappearing from many resorts. At Seaview, Isle of Wight, in 1902 they had been replaced by tents.

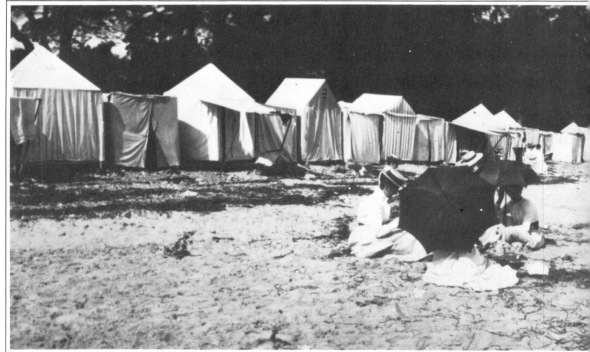

Right
The fun element of a
beach holiday is
expressed in this
photograph of 1910.
The parasol was an
inheritance from that
interest in Japanese art
which influenced such
artists as Whistler and
Degas.

On the Sands under the East Cliff, Bournemouth.

Above
The variety and elegance of the
costumes worn by these bathers on
the Isle of Wight suggests that they
belonged to that class of society which
spent their holidays yachting at
Cowes or Bembridge

Left
Timid swimmers were given a
feeling of confidence by a rope tied
firmly round their waists, or by
clinging to one attached to their
bathing machine. This illustration
of a swimming class in Brighton
dates from the 1870s

Below, left
Paddling in the rock pools was spiced with the delights of discovering the flora and fauna of the sea.

Below
French and British seabathing habits contrasted. A cartoon from the weekly magazine *Judy*, August 1882.

Bottom
On the beach at Aberdeen, 1912.

The Beach, Aberdeen

The
Social Round

THE early Victorians who went to the seaside were very class conscious. They took with them the manners and social codes of the old spas, where the gentry and upper classes had dictated the form. Even after the railways began bringing the ordinary Englishman and his family to the seaside, a distinct social code separated the sedate (and perhaps even rather bored?) upper classes from the much more boisterous working classes. As late as the early Edwardian period, middle-class ladies would never be seen paddling in the sea, for instance; only their maids, or the children's nannies, could do something so undignified.

Those who saw themselves as better than ordinary folk kept themselves to themselves. A visitor to Ramsgate in 1864 noticed that 'those highly respectable seaside visitors who have apartments in the terraces and crescents, and prefer keeping apart from the regular mob of holiday people, generally congregate on the sands near the Pier. They take their money's worth out of their penny chair ... and bring work or a novel from the circulating library with them.' At Brighton, the more respectable people kept to the West Pier, leaving the Palace Pier to the more noisy day trippers. For some, the big resorts became too noisy and vulgar, and they moved away altogether, from Brighton to sedate Hove, from Blackpool to quiet Lytham St Anne's, even from summer to winter at Torquay, where the major Season was after the tourists had gone home in September, or across to the Isle of Wight where even the popular resorts, like Sandown and Ventnor, never became big and brash like some on the mainland.

Most resorts could be seen at a glance to fit into a recognizable, nicely differentiated social scale.

'You judge of the manners of a town by its customs,' noted a writer in the ILLUSTRATED TIMES in 1856. 'Margate is what is termed vulgar, that is to say, it does not wear gloves, never dresses before dinner, and likes hot rum-and-water with lemon in it. It is Ramsgate smoking a clay pipe, with its coat and boots off. . . .

'Margate makes a fine noise if its dinner isn't ready at one, whilst Ramsgate takes an early lunch at the same hour, and Broadstairs rings the bell to have the breakfast things taken away. They consume a vast quantity of ardent spirits at Margate, but at Ramsgate bottled beer is in fashion, and at Broadstairs a bottle of sherry will last for three dinners. We're told that Margate is a "jolly place", that Ramsgate is a "genteel town", and Broadstairs a "dull and grand watering place", and, no doubt, if everybody says so, the definitions must be correct.'

If they stayed in the big resorts, respectable folk were inclined to retreat from the bazaars and public assembly rooms to the drawing-rooms of their terraces and crescents or to the elegant public rooms of the grand hotels which began appearing about the 1860s. Dancing masters 'from Mayfair' or men like 'Mr Watson, Drill Sergeant' at Scarborough in 1881, began advertising their willingness to lend their experience at private parties and assemblies.

Even the lists of names and addresses of visitors which appeared in local newspapers came in time to emphasise the exclusiveness of the upper classes. The lists covered the grand hotels and smart addresses of a town and grew longer and longer, often taking up two or three pages on a large-format newspaper from the end of August until November, when they began to peter out with the ending of the fashionable season. It was not really done for the fashionable to appear at a resort in July or August when the *hoi poloi* and families with children on holiday from school were in the ascendant. The lists had disappeared from most newspapers by the end of the century.

Despite this air of exclusiveness with which the well-to-do surrounded themselves, the social forms they clung to were generally followed by all who stayed for any length of time at the seaside.

The highlight of the day for everyone was not the morning bathe which, indeed, few people really enjoyed, or the sitting on the beach, but the afternoon promenade. Throughout the century, the walk about the town, and particularly along the seafront, was an essential part of the life of a resort. Everyone came out to see and be seen, the rich in their carriages, on their horses and, later, in their motors, the rest on foot, but all dressed in their finest.

When Mrs Brown, working-class heroine of Arthur Sketchley's series of popular sixpenny novels, packed for Brighton in the 1870s, her neighbour advised her to take something dark-coloured, 'as would make you look like a duchess through everyone bein' that dressy in Brighton, as them dark colours as throws out your figger again the sea in walking on the promenade.' But Mrs Brown is an honest man's wife, with no desire to look like a duchess, 'so I shall wear my own things as will be a meriner and a Paisley shawl.'

The Victorian seaside visitor was very clothes-conscious. Those huge trunks and leather grips with which everyone travelled were packed with new clothes, probably lighter and slightly less formal than those they wore in town. Ladies wore their crinolines and round hats—surely the least practical costume imaginable on windy coasts and damp sands—as long as they were fashionable and then in the 1870s exchanged them for tight corsetting and bustles. Young men tried to get a nautical, or at least exotic, flavour into their seaside dress. By the time Edward VII came to the throne, they would be appearing in all the glory of shiny new straw boaters, blazers more richly striped than Joseph's Coat, gay belts or cumberbunds, and white flannels.

Many local newspapers ran regular fashion notes. The SCARBOROUGH GAZETTE, for instance, went so far as to reprint the fashion notes from the ENGLISH WOMAN'S DOMESTIC MAGAZINE which described current fashionable seaside wear in detail.

This emphasis on dress, and the importance of wearing the right clothes, highlights the fact that for most Victorians and Edwardians, the seaside was something special. It meant an escape from everyday working life.

One could forget life in the towns and, with a bit of planning, one could become someone more important at a seaside resort where one was unknown.

In the 1870s, the music hall entertainer George Leybourne was singing about 'The Heavy Swell of the Sea' who was 'a prince of nautical swells' at the seaside but measured ribbon in a draper's shop back home. Vesta Tilley used the same theme in several of her Edwardian era songs, and Ada Reeve sang of 'the flashy-dressed young fellow whose pa you know's an Earl–by the sea!'

This was one game the respectable middle classes, clustered elegantly round the bandstand, could play as well as the drapers' assistants, millinery apprentices and shopgirls on the sands. 'Holiday time was a land of pretence; they all laid claim to a social status they did not possess and nobody believed anyone, but it was part of the fun,' wrote W. Macqueen-Pope, recalling his late-Victorian childhood in TWENTY SHILLINGS IN THE POUND. 'The men were all in professions, or were naval or military officers on leave. If they were clean-shaven in an age of moustaches, they said they were actors. The girls were all of great wealth and family.'

On the sands at Blackpool, 1845. Although by this date visitors had been coming to Blackpool for the benefits of the seabathing for a hundred years, the place was still very small, with only Mr. Cocker's Victoria Street Assembly Rooms, built in 1837, providing public entertainment on any scale.

'You Can Do a Lot of Things at the Seaside You Can't Do In Town,' sang Mark Sheridan, perhaps having in mind all those flirtations and rowdy revels which were other aspects of seaside life. Just as people could pretend at the seaside to a higher station in life than they actually enjoyed, so too they could be more free and easy in their manners than convention generally permitted.

Early Victorian ladies on an unidentified beach.

Not everyone approved of the free and easy manners of seaside visitors. Day trippers and excursionists, particularly, were the target for much criticism from local people who disliked seeing their town's reputation tarnished by raffish and often drunken crowds. Most day trippers were working-class people who could not afford a long stay at a resort and took advantage of cheap rail and steamer fares on Sundays and on the increased number of one-day holidays given them by the Bank Holiday Act of 1871, to have a change at the resort nearest their town.

To Brighton and back for 3s 6d was a temptation few Londoners could withstand, and Brighton on a Sunday, instead of being at its most calm, became noisy and rackety. Gin shops and public houses were crowded with cockney tourists, and in back slums 'pot-house windows opened upon scenes of coarse enjoyment'.

A Graduate of the University of London, writing about the Brighton Sunday in 1861, said that the town's experience of the past season, when the Brighton and South Coast Railway Company had run excursions to Brighton, had 'surely proved offensive enough to the inhabitants of Brighton to induce them to remonstrate with the Company in order to prevent a repetition of those disgraceful scenes which were enacted in many parts of the town.'

Alas for the Graduate and the inhabitants of Brighton, excursion trains had come to stay, and Brighton would have to endure many more Sundays when the Queens Road would swarm 'with drunken and disorderly persons, who set aside all decency and whose conduct was an offence against public morals. . . . Many were left behind from their trains. . . . The carriages were filled with young men and women, in too many cases inflamed with strong drink, whose conversation was disgusting enough to shock every sense of propriety. . . .' Many of those who had missed their trains would spend the night on the beach, the lucky ones finding a bathing machine to sleep in. Many others would find themselves in court accused of minor crimes, among the most frequent of which were assaulting landladies, shop-lifting and kissing ladies in dark tunnels.

Steamer excursionists were not always much better, judging by an ironic account of a return from Margate in 1856:

'We had had enough of Margate, and left by the four o'clock boat, which was also very closely packed. Several of the excursionists employed their two hours on shore by slaking their thirst; indeed, we met two of them on the parade with their waistcoats undone, and their cravats twisted who would, we should think, never be thirsty again. One of them, who was walking sideways like a crab, vowed that "he must take his old gal something from the seaside"; on which his companion suggests "a pen'orth of Happles" as a suitable present, and one not likely to be met with in London. . . . We had a very pleasant trip home, and everybody was very free and easy and happy. A passenger who had evidently had more to drink than to eat at dinner, got into a coil of cable, and fell asleep like a bird in its nest; another took off his boots, which were tight, and dozed in his socks.'

The local councils of some of the more select resorts did their best to discourage the day tripper, and passed regulations making the local Sunday as unexciting as possible. A ban on Sunday trains at Bournemouth was not lifted until 1914, and steamer trips on Sundays were not scheduled there until the end of the 1920s. Many resorts forbade band-playing on Sundays in the gardens and on the esplanades, and piers were also closed.

At Bridlington in the 1880s, the local board began to reflect the hardening of attitude, not to say social hypocrisy, which characterised much of late-Victorian society. They came down hard on street musicians in an Act of 1889 which provided that any householder could tell any street musician or singer to move away from his neighbourhood, on pain of a penalty not exceeding 40 shillings. The board also contemplated closing public houses on Sundays and forbidding the performance of even sacred music by the Parade Band on the same day. 'Anti-Humbug' wrote to the BRIDLINGTON GAZETTE protesting at these high-handed attempts at regulating the morals of visitors and residents at Bridlington.

In contrast, the picture postcard, which began appearing in the 1890s reflected a much more friendly approach. Postcard designers liked to show pretty girls on their cards. But their pretty girls were not the well-brought-up young women with geologist's hammers, crochet work or library books in their hands usually depicted by the magazines and newspapers of the 1850s and 1860s. The turn-of-the-century girl was often shown being kissed by a young man, or even several young men. She was a much gayer and more easy-going creature altogether, who did not hesitate to show a shapely leg under her hitched-up skirt.

Not that the girls of earlier generations had been completely without relaxed attitudes at the seaside. For some time it was fashionable to wear the hair hanging loose, in a way which would have raised eyebrows in town. And it was not difficult to get away from mama long enough to meet a young man in the bazaars or spa gardens. Perhaps mama turned a blind eye in the hope that her daughter had found an eligible suitor, for the seaside had inherited from the watering place the reputation for being a marriage market, or at least a place to have flirtations with the opposite sex, which was still undimmed at the end of the century. It was a reputation which added an extra spice to the already numerous attractions of the seaside.

A forest of parasols and top hats on the promenade
at Brighton, *c.* 1864.

Above
Fashionable Scarborough in the
season, as shown to the readers of
The Illustrated London News in
October 1871. The magazine
admitted that this scene could
scarcely have been witnessed later
than mid-August as 'the period
available for alfresco repose and
social converse has already passed
for this year.'

Top right
A shrimp stall and customers on
Margate Pier, *c.* 1902.
Right
The beach at Brighton, drawn by
Miss Runciman for *The Illustrated
London News* in 1859. Brighton
'may be said to have reached the
zenith of popularity as a watering
place,' remarked the magazine, 'and
nowhere has the extravagance and
irrationality of costume been carried
to greater excess.'

Right
The King's Gardens in Southport, opened in 1913 by George V. To the right is the Water Chute opened in 1903 and the Maxim Flying Machine, designed by Sir Hiram Maxim of machine-gun fame, which began operating about 1906.

Below
Flirtation on the beach at Yarmouth, photographed by Paul Martin in the early 1890s. Martin used the new hand camera to good effect, hiding it in a black leather case, so that his subjects never suspected that the eye of the camera was upon them.

Left
It must have been a
cold day at Blackpool
when these donkeys and
their well-wrapped
potential riders were
photographed in 1903.
Below
Paddling at Hastings in
the 1890s.

Most Invigorating!

My word! What a splendid catch.

THE LOVERS SEAT. HASTINGS.

Facing page, top
Same gentlemen, different ladies.
Two postcards from Davidson
Bros' Real Photographic Series
with seaside flirtations as their
theme.
Facing page, bottom
'How do you like the view. I am
enjoying myself A1,' wrote Lilian to
her friend Florrie on the back of this
picture of herself and a gentleman
friend on Hastings popular Lovers'
Seat.
Right
Sheet music of the 1870s. George
Leybourne sang 'with immense
success' several songs about social
life at the seaside.
Below
A postcard of 1908, taking a tilt at
the laws passed by some local
authorities inhibiting seaside
pleasures.

Above
A choice of refreshments – shell fish or 'pure ices' for visitors to Brighton at the turn of the century.

Right
Rowing out to the boat: members of the Bembridge Sailing Club and their ladies, 1908.

Far right, bottom
Earnest conversation on a bench at Scarborough:
'It is easy to tell as they stroll on the pier,
  And glance at the boats and the sea,
That the youth and the maiden are wanting a skiff,
  A row and a chat by themselves on the sea,
  A chat by themselves on the sea.'
Verse by O. Zone in *A Pictorial Souvenir of Scarborough* (1898).

Above
Ladies often wore
coloured veils to protect
their eyes from the sun.
These rowers were at
the Bembridge Sailing
Club, Isle of Wight, in
1908.

Facing page
Their clothes indicating their poverty, this man and his child pose for the camera, *c.* 1910. The camera used was a folding pocket Kodak.

Facing page, inset
Smiles for the camera from Lil and her daughters, 1913.

Above
Showing a leg at Ramsgate.

Right
A family party, not looking very comfortable, on the beach in 1907.

Facing page, top
A Bleriot monoplane, hired by the *Daily Mail*, at
Tenby in 1914. The aeroplane trailed a banner
advertising the newspaper, which issued numbered
tickets with its copies on the day of the visit, the
holder of the lucky number being given a free
flight.
Facing page, bottom
A page from *Judy*, September 6, 1882,
celebrating the sea.
Below
Watching the day's catch brought in, *c.* 1902.

Having
a Lovely Time

MOST seaside resorts in Victorian and Edwardian Britain, even the smallest among them, offered their visitors more than just the simple delights of clean, fresh air, sand and salt water. These may have been sufficient attractions for the sick and convalescent who congregated in the quieter resorts, but for the vast majority of holidaymakers, the seaside provided a marvellous array of entertainments and activities for which the sand and sea merely provided the backdrop and scenic props.

In the early days of their growth, seaside resorts carried on the traditions of the spas, and enterprising local people established Circulating Libraries and Assembly Rooms where society could gather to gossip, dance, match-make and take part in innocent raffles where the gambler might win a packet of pins, a cake of soap or–if he or she were lucky–a silver card-case or a plated tea-kettle.

In a remarkably short time, the libraries and assembly rooms of the more popular resorts far outgrew their modest origins and were replaced by the fantastic Winter Gardens, Spas and Kursaals which were the pride and joy of the late nineteenth-century resorts. Few people visiting Blackpool in 1841, for instance, when the town's population was only 2,168 could have envisaged that by the end of the century it would have had as just one of many attractions a Winter Garden capable of accommodating ten times that many people in its Floral Hall, Grand Pavilion, Empress Ballroom, Opera House, skating rink, tea rooms and gardens.

The pursuit of pleasure soon moved beyond the confines of the assembly rooms and concert halls out into the streets, along the first piers, and onto the sands, where minstrels and Punch and Judy held sway, and where at night the darkness was lightened by fireworks displays, illuminations, and the Chinese lanterns which lit the paths of innumerable parks and gardens.

There was always something to do, see or hear: the camera obscura and, late in the century, the penny peep show to wonder at; flowers to admire in splendid Italian Gardens or Lovers' Walks; lectures and concerts to listen to; balloon ascents and – just before World War I put a temporary halt to the fun – aeroplanes to watch landing on the smooth sands; flower battles and dancing to enjoy at the end of the pier; galas, regattas, fairs, balls – a never-ending round of events throughout the long Victorian summers.

As the century wore on, resorts began to cater for sports-loving holidaymakers, and from the late 1880s guide books referred increasingly to the many excellent facilities for tennis, golf, badminton, cycling, boating and other sports provided for the visitor, and hotels which could boast of tennis courts in their grounds were considered to have scored over their rivals.

Much of this activity had a musical accompaniment for the Victorian seaside resort was a constant medley of sounds, musical and vocal, day and night. Street singers and musicians vied with bell-ringing town criers, muffinmen and sweet sellers for the attention of passers-by, and the Punch and Judy man was as likely to set up his booth in the main street as on the sands.

Here is Margate at the height of the 1856 season: 'Street music was so plentiful that had we given to each performer, a penny for ten yards would not have cleared us. . . . A poor old tenor, with one high note, which he gave as often as possible, was singing to a harmonium accompaniment, under the balcony of a lodging house; further on a man with an accordion was writhing like an eel as he played to a singing boy who was killing himself with Scotch ballads, whilst at the corner of the street an organ man with a powerful wrist sent out such volumes of sound, that for the moment we also wished that, in the same way as chimneys are ordered to consume their own smoke, street organs might be made to consume their own music.'

In the letters, diaries, novels and newspapers of the

period, it is hard to find anyone who appreciated this cacophony of sound which disturbed the seaside peace from an early hour on fine days. Charles Dickens' frustrations at Broadstairs are well known. He wrote to his friend John Forster in 1847: 'Vagrant music is getting to that height here, and is so impossible to be escaped from, that I fear Broadstairs and I must part company in time to come. Unless it pours of rain, I cannot write half an hour without the most excruciating organs, fiddles, bells or glee singers. There is a violin of the most torturing kind under the window now (Time, ten in the morning) and an Italian box of music on the steps—both in full blast.'

Apart from this impromptu music, regular band concerts, black minstrel shows and concert parties played a major part in the musical life of many resorts. At first, the minstrels dominated the scene, as much for the style of their music as for their blacked-up faces. The first minstrel troupe came to England from America in 1843. This was the 'Ethiopian band' called the Virginian Minstrels who had caused such a stir in New York with their blackened faces and plantation songs. Their style was soon to be copied by groups all over the country, and the rattle of the bones, the clatter of the tambourines and the twanging of the banjo became an essential part of the seaside atmosphere for half a century.

Many of the minstrel groups gave themselves names incorporating the words 'Christy Minstrels' hoping to benefit from the renown of the great American Edwin P. Christy, although he himself never appeared in Britain. The famous Moore and Burgess Minstrels, who gave their last performance at St Leonards' Pavilion in June 1900, started out as the 'Moore and Burgess Christy Minstrels' but dropped the name 'Christy' in the early 1870s. After the original groups from America had left the scene, few, if any, of the many minstrels singing about going home to Dixie or being way down upon the Swanee River were either black or American. Behind the cork ash blacking, the faces were all home-grown. Harry Reynolds, in his MINSTREL MEMORIES, wrote that the best corks for 'black face' were those from champagne bottles, burnt to ash and mixed to a paste with water. Champagne? It is hard to believe that those groups of itinerant musicians, performing several hours daily on the sands, dodging the tides, and passing round a tin for pennies among spectators who were not obliged to give any, drank enough champagne to keep themselves well supplied with cork even if, in those golden days, champagne was comparatively cheap. Probably they had special arrangements with waiters and hotel-keepers.

The years around 1900 saw the surprisingly swift demise of the minstrel show. After half a century of dominance, they were almost swept away by a flood of Pierrot groups and concert parties.

The Pierrot troupes' appearance in the early 1890s helped confirm the increasingly respectable status of seaside entertainers, who were gradually throwing off the street busker taint of earlier years. At the seaside, those who in town considered the music hall at best dubious entertainment, found the 'refined', 'family' entertainment provided by the concert parties and Pierrot shows reassuringly safe.

The first Pierrot group in England was the inspiration of a well-known banjoist, Clifford Essex. His 'Pierrot Banjo Band' first performed at Henley Regatta and Cowes Regatta in 1891, and in 1892, now called the 'Royal Pierrots', they toured the seaside resorts of the South Coast. Soon the Pierrot's baggy white suit with its black pompoms was one of the most popular sights in most seaside resorts.

One of *Punch* artist John Leech's favourite themes was the seaside. In this 1847 cartoon, he jokes at the expense of seaside libraries and the young ladies, sea-drenched hair straggling under their bonnets, who frequented them.

THE SEA-SIDE CIRCULATING LIBRARY.

'ALL THE NEW WORKS ARE OUT, MISS. BUT HERE'S THE SECOND VOLUME OF THE 'SCOTTISH CHIEFS'—OR HERE'S 'CAMPBELL'S PHILOSOPHY OF RHETORIC' IF YOU WOULD LIKE TO READ THAT."

A minstrel band on the beach at Brighton, *c.* 1870. The Punch-like figure to the right appears to owe his costume as much to Italian pantomime as to American black minstrelry.

Alongside the Pierrot group, the concert party also flourished, with similar programmes of songs, music and variety acts, but with rather smarter costumes than the generations-old Pierrot outfit: evening dress or nautical-style suits with brass buttons and peaked caps were common.

Later, as they became established and moved up the social scale, the best concert parties gave up their al fresco shows on the sands or in public gardens for the permanent stages of pier pavilions, concert halls and kursaals. Many famous performers who were to grace the English theatre in later years got their grounding in stage craft from these concert parties. W. H. Berry, an attraction at London's Adelphi Theatre for many years, had six years' training on Yarmouth's Wellington Pier followed by four years as an original member of the well-known Broadstairs Bohemian Concert Party before the impresario George Edwardes noticed his talents and whisked him off to London. Leslie Henson, Bobby Howes, Max Miller,

Stanley Holloway, even screen idol Ronald Colman, and many London music hall artists whose names were household words, began their careers at the seaside. (Many of them often returned to the seaside, under assumed names, when they were 'resting' from the London stage.)

Sometimes, players who had started out on the halls, found their greatest fame on the sands. One such was Harry Gold, of Irish descent and born in Jersey in 1866, who was well known in music halls as a singer of sentimental Irish songs when, at the age of 31, he went to Ramsgate and started a beach entertainment. He began with a stage of planks near the East Pier, and in time his company was supporting groups in several resorts in England and Wales. He had been twenty-five years in Ramsgate and Margate before he forsook his caravan and built a permanent stage.

At this time, there was technically no such thing as municipal entertainment, apart from the public band concerts, which were a major feature of all seaside entertainment programmes, for it was not until after World War I that an Act of Parliament gave local authorities the power to risk public money on entertainments.

Naturally enough, though, local authorities were keenly interested in promoting the prosperity of their towns and were generally closely involved in all sorts of schemes for attracting visitors. 'Entertainments managers', whose job it was to oversee the arrangements for the band concerts, flower battles and fireworks displays which delighted visitors every year, usually came within the local government orbit in some way. Pre-war Ramsgate, for instance, had an Entertainments Association, the members of which were all Council members who had made a personal guarantee against possible loss.

For as many resorts as could manage to build one, the pier was the outstanding attraction, providing entertainment on a lavish scale for all who cared to pay the twopence or so entrance fee. The bandstand might be free and the major social gathering place of a resort, but a ticket to the pier was a passport to another world.

THERE ARE SOME NICE PIERROTS AND OTHER FUNNY PEOPLE HERE! WHEN ARE YOU COMING?

SCARBOROUGH PIERROTS

Facing page, top
A troupe of Pierrots in 1908. 'Had a
huge success last night ... Everyone
says we absolutely knock the
"Follies" into a cocked hat!' said
the note on the back of this card. If
the writer was referring to the
famous Pierrot group started by the
Baddeley brothers in the mid-1890s,
he was probably exaggerating: the
Follies was amongst the best groups.

Facing page, centre
'Weather and tide permitting', most
Pierrot groups gave three or more
shows a day.

Facing page, bottom
Will Catlin was a big name among
Pierrot shows, starting out on the
sands at Scarborough in 1896. By
the time this group was
photographed there in 1905, Catlin's
Pierrots were performing at their
own theatres in Scarborough,
Colwyn Bay and Llandudno.

Below
A group of minstrels on the beach at
Broadstairs *c.* 1912.

Above, top
'NO VULGARITY' was the slogan of
this concert party, photographed at
Herne Bay. They were called The
Bohemians, perhaps to give
themselves some of the cachet of the
well-known Broadstairs Bohemians.

Above
Gilbert Rogers' 'Jovial Jesters'
giving a good twopence-worth at
Rhyl in North Wales.

Above, top
A concert party at Brighton,
c. 1914. Only the deck-chair patrons
paid to watch a concert party; no-
one else was obliged to put money in
the tin, so a good 'bottler' (collector)
was an invaluable asset for any
concert party.

Above
Two girls giving of their best for
Walker's Variety Entertainments at
Southport in Whit Week, 1899.

1794 Deal The Bandstand and Pier

Above
A band concert at Deal, *c.* 1908.

Right
Cover from the programme of a
concert at the Winter Gardens,
Blackpool, in 1897.

Facing page, top
Electric light lends an extra
enchantment to this evening band
concert in the Municipal Gardens,
Southport, in 1899.

Facing page, bottom
A sand artist at work on the beach
at Torquay.

Below
The Punch and Judy booth was a
favourite attraction at the seaside
from the mid-nineteenth century.

Left
Top-hatted elegance for the Company's Band at the Spa, Scarborough, conducted by Charles Godfrey Jr., in 1893.

Facing page, bottom
Julian Kändt's famous band of truly Germanic splendour at the New Spa, Bridlington, 1910.

Below
Taken from a stereoscopic view card of the period, this picture shows the First Parade band, Bridlington, in 1876. This band was led by Professor J. M. Wilson, who had been arranging Promenade Concerts in the town since the 1860s.

Below
Blackpool's famous Tower, opened in 1894, and the Big Wheel, opened in 1896. The Tower still stands as a monument to Victorian 'think big', but the Big Wheel was never a financial success and was pulled down in 1928.

Facing page, top
The Aerial Flight at Southport was a great attraction. Built in 1895 it was taken down in 1911.

Facing page, centre
Scarborough's answer to the Blackpool Tower was this revolving tower, erected in 1898 by the Warwick Revolving Tower Company. It was demolished in 1907.

Facing page, bottom
A postcard of the sands at Skegness, sent in July 1906. The costumes suggest the photograph was taken much earlier.

Aerial Flight, Southport

THE SANDS, SKEGNESS.

A Stroll
Along the Pier

THE seaside pleasure pier began as a landing place for steamers and Channel packets, quickly became a fashionable promenade, and at the height of its glory in early Edwardian days, was the greatest attraction any resort could boast of possessing.

'A good pier has long been regarded as an essential to a seaside town,' said a Brighton guide book in the 1890s, 'and structures of this kind have been erected at nearly every health resort on the coast, some with little pretension to elegance or comfort, mere promenades and landing stages, others of beautiful design and offering superior accommodation.'

At the turn of the century, dozens of piers pushed out into the waters round the coast of Britain. Many of them would undoubtedly have been looked down upon by the writer of the Brighton guide, conscious of the superior attractions of his town's piers. But even a 'mere landing stage' like Brodick Pier on Arran, with its delicate webbing of three arches beneath its deck, had a special kind of charm, unique to the seaside. Of all the buildings – pavilions, spas, bandstands and bazaars – which were part of the Victorian and Edwardian seaside picture, only the pier could not have existed anywhere else.

Most piers were the work of engineers, rather than fashionable architects, although some of the great names of the day were involved in their construction. Thomas Telford designed the first pier at Herne Bay, opened in 1832; Sir John Rennie was responsible for Margate's splendid stone pier, which cost £100,000 to build; and Isambard Kingdom Brunel designed the railway lines which came to be laid down Clevedon Pier in Somerset, although the pier itself had no special engineer, being built in 1869 from components in a factory and assembled on the site. Eugenius Birch's name deserves to be more famous than it is; an engineer from Westminster, he was consultant engineer on Brighton's Chain Pier, designed the Margate Jetty, completed in 1855, and Brighton's West Pier, and was also responsible for the aquaria at Brighton and Scarborough.

Few piers could match in design the graceful silhouettes of the suspension piers at Brighton and Seaview, on the Isle of Wight. Rather, with their wooden decks balanced on ranks of slender iron piles, they had the spindly elegance of storks, treading delicately out to sea.

Close-up, the impression of elegance which made the pier silhouette so distinctive a part of many sea-fronts, gave way to an exuberant Victorian design which embellished pier rails, balconies, seats, pavilions and lamp-standards with marvellously inventive wrought-iron work, wooden filigree edgings, oriental domes and spires, curling dolphins and sea-serpents, fish and anchors. Much of the design style on the Victorian pier had an obvious Oriental or Eastern influence, derived largely from that eighteenth-century interest in Oriental styles which reached its apotheosis with the Prince Regent's Pavilion at Brighton, but partly, too, from the more traditional naval style which had put richly designed figure-heads on the prows of ships.

Some of the most celebrated promenade piers were built in the 1860s by which time most of the major resorts were well established. The piers generally began as simple promenades leading to landing-stages, but when their commercial potential was realised, they were extended and enlarged to make room for pavilions, theatres, bazaars and kiosks. Brighton's West Pier for instance, was conceived by Eugenius Birch as a vast promenade, the surface area of its deck covering 39,000 feet and stretching 1,115 feet out to sea. From the day it was opened in October 1866, it was immensely popular with the public, who flocked through the turnstiles in their thousands, taking the air and enjoying the music of the band playing at the pierhead. But the promenade was not enough, and by the time the pier was extensively rebuilt

On the Chain Pier, Brighton. An illustration from an 1862 guide to Brighton.

in 1894, it included a new landing-stage for boats, a handsome pavilion which could hold 1,500 people, and accommodation for many kinds of side-shows.

Clacton-on-Sea boasted only one house in 1852, but by 1873 had grown large enough to open its own pier, which was extended many times and had a pavilion added in the 1890s. The first pier at Southend was opened in 1830, and was rammed six times by ships. It was rebuilt in 1889, and was extended several times until, at 7,080 feet, it was the longest pleasure pier in the world. The pier at St Anne's-on-Sea was another which began as a simple promenade pier in 1889 and was enlarged to include a pavilion twenty years later.

The seaside pier knew its greatest glory at the turn of the century. No longer just a place for an elegant stroll, it had become the focus of all the fun, frivolity, thrills and excitement sought after by Edwardians released on holiday from their stuffy offices, teeming factories and quiet suburban homes. The camera obscura, which had given thousands of visitors intriguing glimpses of the sand and distant coast-lines, had been out-moded by the penny-in-the-slot machines, some of which gave wide-eyed lads and lasses even more intriguing glimpses of the naughty things the butler saw, and others of which disgorged neat little tin boxes of chocolates and sweets for children. Electric light had replaced gas, and the fairy lights, like those which outlined the arches and roof-tops of Brighton's Palace Pier from the night it was opened in 1899, out-rivalled in splendour the colours of the fireworks displays which were regular pierhead attractions.

In fact, everyone got good value out of the piers. Their owners, whether private companies like the Coast Development Company which owned the piers at Felixstowe, Clacton and Walton-on-the-Naze for many years, or the shareholders of Brighton's West Pier who were paid dividends averaging eight per cent per annum throughout the 1880s, or public bodies like the Southend Local Board which was far-sighted enough to acquire the Southend Pier in 1875, were profiting by them. And the visitors had splendid value for their twopences.

Even when the twopence had bought little more than a stroll in the bracing sea air, it had been worth the money. It had taken the seaside visitor far out to sea into the brisk atmosphere of the oceans, where his romantic Victorian soul could indulge all sorts of notions of adventure on the high seas and of the mysteries of the deep, while he remained free of worries about seasickness and storms. From the pierhead he could have an unrivalled view of the town front and the coastline. He could even indulge the most satisfying seaside pleasure of all: catching fish.

By the 1890s, the value of the twopenny pier ticket was stupendous.

Take the Promenade Pier at Ramsgate, for instance. Admission to the pier was twopence for adults and one penny for children, and entitled the visitor to take part in all the amenities of the pier. In the mornings, one could watch Miss Lizzie Beckwith give diving and swimming exhibitions at the pierhead, or one could listen to an open-air concert or variety performance. In the evenings, there would be a concert at the pier pavilion, which held about 250 people, half of whom could stand at the rear of the hall, without charge, other than the cost of the programme. An average concert night might include a soubrette, a male vocalist, an acrobatic juggler, a red-nosed comedian, a lightning cartoonist, a burlesque

Children looking at the penny-in-the-slot machines on Brighton's West Pier, 1901.

instrumentalist, a lady vocalist specialising in operatic numbers, a dame comedian, and some lively sketches. After the concert, there would be dancing, confetti and flower battles, and perhaps a fireworks display.

Miss Lizzie Beckwith, 'of the famous aquatic family', was an example of an extraordinary breed of entertainers who used the sea as their prop. 'Professors' whose profession was diving off piers were familiar figures at many resorts. At Southport, the crowds at the pierhead gasped in horrified delight as Professor Osbourne dived from frightful heights into the sea. At Brighton, Professor Reddish added charm to his performance by riding off the West Pier on a bicycle. In 1890 the West Pier had as an attraction Miss Minnie Johnson, who gave a daily performance in a tank. One Wednesday afternoon she accomplished the feat of swimming from the Chain Pier to the West Pier in 36 minutes, 25 seconds. 'On landing at the Pier, she showed little sign of fatigue,' noted the BRIGHTON HERALD's reporter.

The pleasure-seeking tripper could spend a great deal more than twopence on the pier, of course. Even before the hectic days of the 1890s, many piers had had little

shops and stalls. Brighton's Chain Pier, the first of the pleasure piers, had small shops built into the hollow iron towers above its piles. By 1861 the Chain Pier Bazaar was a major attraction in the town, offering many charming novelties. Ladies—or their husbands—could buy 'articles of jewellery of the most *recherché* kind'. There were French and German toys for the children, pocket books, work-boxes, the celebrated Fire-proof China, fancy baskets, walking sticks, combs and brushes, stereoscopic slides, and books and stationery. Print-sellers, shell ornament stalls and Mrs Snelling, 'artist in wax flowers', all clamoured for the visitor's custom. Tiring of them, he could test his weight on a correct Weighing Machine and Standard, with cards of weight and height, he could pay sixpence for admission to the Royal Camera Obscura, which embraced a view of the coast from Worthing to Newhaven, or he could even get away altogether on a steamer from the pierhead.

As the guide books said, there was little the pier could not offer the ladies and gentlemen of Victorian and Edwardian Britain in the way of elegance, comfort and superior accommodation.

The Chain Pier, Brighton, was designed on the same principles as the suspension bridge, and built on four massive iron-clad piles. It was opened in 1823 and was a prominent feature of the town, appearing in paintings by Turner and Constable, until it was destroyed in a storm in 1896.

Palace Pier, Evening, Brighton.

5 SEA VIEW (Isle of Wight). — The Pier. — LL.

Above, top
The Marine Palace Pier opened in
1899, the third and last pier to be
built at Brighton.

Above
The pier at Seaview, Isle of Wight,
was the second suspension pier to be
built in England. Opened in 1880, it
had curved decks suspended
between four sets of pillars.

Ryde I.W.

Above, top
Left high and dry by the tide, Rhyl
Pier displays the elegant structure
of its iron pillars. The pier was built
in 1867 and the pavilion at its
entrance was added in 1891.

Above
The pier at Ryde, Isle of Wight, is
three piers in one: the Old Pier,
which dates back to 1814, the
Tramway Pier and the Railway
Pier.

Lowestoft

You do not
mention the
pier card I
hope it
arrived in
The parcel.
It is funny
you did not
get it for so
long. Will
you let me
know what
you did with
I have found
your letter.
Love pu.

The Pier and Sands

The Pavilion, Colwyn Bay.

56785. JM

JETTY & PALACE STEAMER, MARGATE

The Pier Clacton-on-Sea

AMERICAN BOWLING SALOON

Weston-Super-Mare from Pavilion

Facing page, top
Margate's jetty, begun in the 1850s, replacing an
earlier structure, provided a new landing stage.

Facing page, centre
Steamer traffic between London and Ipswich
helped almost unknown Clacton to a rapid rise to
prominence once it had opened its pier in 1873. The
pier was enlarged and extended several times until
it was over 1200 feet long.

Facing page, bottom
The promenade on Weston-super-Mare's splendid
Grand Pier, built in 1903-4, carried a pavilion, with
a hall able to seat 2000 people, a bandstand, kiosk
and shops.

Below
Eastbourne Pier showing an American influence.
The pier was opened in 1872, and a pavilion and
concert hall were added in 1888.

This page, top
Plymouth Harbour in
the 1890s. The pier was
opened in 1884.
Right
The promenaders here
setting out along
Southend Pier had a
long way to go to the
pierhead: the world's
longest promenade pier
grew to 7,080 feet.
Facing page, top
The end of a long walk:
the pierhead at
Southend.

THE PIERHEAD, SOUTHPORT

THE HIGH DIVE.

PROF. OSBOURNE, HIGH DIVER.

Above
Dancing on Blackpool's Victoria (South) Pier,
c. 1910. The pier was the third and last pier to be
built at Blackpool, and was opened in 1893.

Left
'Professor Osbourne' demonstrating his high dive
at the end of Southport Pier.

Below
Relaxing on the pier at Littlehampton, 1898.
Facing page
The entrance to Blackpool's Central Pier. Called
the South Pier when it was opened in 1868, it had
to be given a different designation when the
Victoria Pier was built south of it.

Seaside
Souvenirs

SEASIDE holidays might be over all too quickly, but the memory of them could linger on, especially if helped along by a souvenir: perhaps a white china mug with 'A Present From Brighton' written in elegant gold script round the middle, a pierced-border plate with a transfer picture of the Blackpool Tower in the centre, a shell-covered box, a stick of lettered rock, or even – though it usually began to smell so horrible so quickly that no one wanted it – the seaweed 'barometer' which had hung from the windowsill of a boarding house bedroom. Whatever the form, the souvenir 'trifles' from dozens of seaside resorts are among the most evocative relics of the Victorian and Edwardian ages left to us.

Some of the most attractive seaside souvenirs were those made by the visitors themselves from the natural resources of the seashore. This was particularly true of the 1850s and 1860s, when a very real interest in the natural history of the coasts drew armies of eager amateur naturalists, marine biologists and zoologists, and conchologists to the water's edge in search of as yet undiscovered wonders of nature.

The results of their labours were turned into elegant sketch books, collections of shells and rock samples, albums and pictures made of pressed seaweeds, and even into small aquaria. They were helped in their work by a steady stream of books written to guide and inform the amateur naturalist.

Among the best of the writers of these books was Philip Henry Gosse, whose attractive and enthusiastically written books inspired hundreds of people to venture into the shallow seas round Britain's coasts, armed with nets, specimen jars, baskets lined with gutta percha, and geologist's hammers searching out the wonders of life in rock pools and tidal shores.

'What if I were to open before you resources that you could never exhaust in the longest life, a fund of intellectual delight that would never satiate; pursuits so enchanting that the more you followed them the more single and ardent would be your love for them . . .' he asked his readers in an early book, SEASIDE PLEASURES, published in 1853. And in book after book, many of them illustrated with his own exquisite drawings of shells, corals, anemones and other creatures he had discovered, he provided just such a fund of delight.

Another outstanding contributor to the cause of amateur naturalism was Mrs Alfred Gatty, whose BRITISH SEAWEEDS, published in 1863, was more than simply a highly competent description of the types of seaweeds to be found round the coasts of Britain. Like Gosse, she communicated a great enthusiasm for her subject. Seaweed collecting, she said, was a pursuit 'which throws a charm over every sea-place on the coast. . . . Only let there be sea, and plenty of low, dark rocks stretching out, peninsular-like, into it; and only let the dinner-hour be fixed for high-water time, and the loving disciple asks no more of fate.'

Seaside landladies may not always have shared her enthusiasm, for the preservation and laying-out of seaweeds called for all sorts of equipment, including bowls, meat-dishes, plenty of sea and fresh water, oil cloths to cover good tables and the carpets, all of which the landlady might be expected to provide, along with the neat's-foot oil which rendered waterpoof the enthusiast's boots.

This great interest in the natural history of the seaside had largely disappeared by the 1870s, most people encountering all the natural history they wanted in the marine aquaria and shell grottoes which were attractions at many resorts.

For the less energetic souvenir-hunter, there were always little remembrances and trifles which could be purchased from local bazaars and shops, or from the itinerant salesmen and women who were always in evidence on beaches and promenades.

Many resorts had their own local souvenir industries, such as the jet jewellery trade at Whitby, the making of glass paperweights and pictures from the coloured sands of Alum Bay on the Isle of Wight, or the animals made from shells which were a speciality of Margate. The Pegwell Bay shrimp became a sought-after delicacy when made into paste and the pots into which it was packed were souvenirs of great charm. Their lids were printed with delicately-coloured views of Ramsgate and the bay in a process perfected by the firm of Pratt of Fenton.

But as the nineteenth century wore on and the seaside became almost an industry in its own right, catering for the needs of thousands of people, so industries grew up which produced wares for sale on a country-wide basis.

One of the earliest was the Scottish firm of Smith of Mauchline, whose attractive transfer-printed objects made out of creamy-yellow sycamore wood graced many a souvenir shop throughout the country and began a vogue which was imitated by other manufacturers. Smiths began producing their inexpensive woodware early in the century, but their products were most popular in the second half of the century. Snuff boxes, pin boxes, pencil cases, brush backs, covers for seaside view albums, needle-cases and other trifles, all printed with transfer pictures of English scenes, seaside resorts and their piers, hotels and familiar landmarks, made long-lasting and pretty souvenirs.

Equally attractive but much more expensive was the turned-wood ware which had been made at Tunbridge Wells in Kent since the seventeenth century. The best of this was decorated with end-grain mosaic and therefore required a craftsman's skill in its manufacture.

Towards the latter part of the century, the amount of souvenirs produced for the holiday trade grew enormously, losing a great deal in quality in the process. The pretty wooden products of Smith of Mauchline came eventually to be imitated cheaply, with stuck-on photographs taking the place of the more delicate transfer printing. The well-known Goss white china, with its detailed reproductions of the crests of towns, cities and important institutions, appeared on a big scale and soon had a number of imitators in Britain and Germany. Most of these imitations lacked the finish and style of the Goss china, and were aimed at the less discriminating tastes of the holiday crowds, who were happy to go home with a tiny white china model of a lighthouse, a boat, a bathing machine, or even a Punch and Judy booth, even if the outlines might be rough and the transfer crookedly applied.

Germany and Austria supplied the British souvenir trade with the majority of its products before the First World War. Much of the pink-mauve transfer-printed china sold at most resorts came from Germany, as did several varieties of heavily-embossed and raised-surface wares, and most of those familiar pierced-border plates. Many albums of seaside views, which were another favourite souvenir of the time, particularly those containing strips of pull-out views, were also of German origin.

The view albums and those other pretty, typically Victorian conceits, pictorial envelopes and writing paper, were precursors of the most popular seaside souvenir of all—the postcard.

From the beginning of the Penny Post in Britain, postcards had to be enclosed in envelopes for addressing

Shrimping on Scarborough Sands, c. 1913.

and posting, but once the Post Office had given up its monopoly in stamped postcards in 1894, the manufacture of pictorial cards which could be sent through the post with a halfpenny stamp affixed, went ahead by leaps and bounds. Postcard collecting became a nation-wide craze, which received an extra fillip in 1902 when it became legal for messages as well as addresses to be written on the backs of cards. By this time, card size had become standardised, so that albums with pages specially slotted to hold postcards could now be manufactured. 'Here is another one for your collection' was as familiar a phrase on the backs of Edwardian cards as 'Having a lovely time' and 'Wish you were here'.

Photography, which had made possible the postcard trade on such a large scale, also gave the seaside another popular souvenir. By the end of Victoria's reign, beach photography had become a fairly quick and simple affair. Tripod cameras, surrounded by stands displaying the results of the photographer's skill, were a feature of most beaches, and children, particularly, seldom went home from a seaside holiday without a photograph of themselves, often mounted in a black frame and held in place by gilt filigree at the corners.

'Valuable Addition to the Aquarium', a cartoon by John Leech published in *Punch* in 1860.

VALUABLE ADDITION TO THE AQUARIUM.

Above
A sand picture, made c. 1845, of the Needles, Isle of Wight.

Below
Coloured sands from Alum Bay in the Isle of Wight were used in these Victorian glass paperweights. They stand six to nine inches high.

Facing page, top
The seaside was a good source of
themes for writers of popular
Victorian songs and dance music.
These two examples of sheet music
depict Margate in the 1860s, with its
famous jetty in the background, and
Brighton in the 1870s.

Facing page, bottom
A Victorian glazed white china
shrimp bowl, of a kind often found
in pierhead tea rooms.

Above, top
Two ornate china cups made in
Germany. *Left*, a gilt-painted cup
with a print of the pier at
Ramsgate. *Right*, 'A present from
Southend-on-Sea', in white heavily-
embossed china with gilt decoration.

Above
A typical example of a white china
pictorial souvenir from Austria, this
teapot was made by Schmidt and
Co. of Carlsbad in Bohemia, who
produced a considerable amount
British souvenir china. The teapot
has a tinted picture of Ventnor, and
is marked on the bottom, 'Victoria,
Austria'.

Above
Pull-out postcards published by Valentine and Sons of Dundee, one of Britian's earliest and largest manufacturers of postcards. These 'mailing novelties', which carried tiny strips of local views under the flaps, were published just before the First World War.

Facing page, top
Bathing costumes on postcards. The skinny gentleman with the monocle was the unlikely subject chosen by 'Jim' in 1908 to carry a note to Mr. Potter-Perkins to ask if he would like Jim to be his valet. The card showing the well-endowed ladies paddling was published by S. Hildesheimer and Co. of London and Manchester and printed in Germany, *c.* 1902-6.

Facing page, bottom
Enjoying a shrimp tea at the Bellevue Tea Gardens, Pegwell Bay, in 1908. Pegwell shrimp paste was a prized delicacy and its manufacture was a flourishing industry from 1760, when it was started by one Samuel Banger, until 1916. It was sold in pots with attractively painted lids which became souvenirs in their own right.

GIRLS! HOW DO YOU LIKE MY FIGURE?

"PADDLING"

Bellevue Tea Gardens, Pegwell Bay.

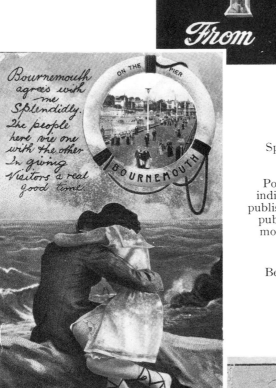

This page and facing page top left
Specific resorts feature on these postcards of
1907-14.
Facing page, top right
Postcard artist Frederick Spurgin seems to be
indicating the start of a new era in this postcard
published in 1914 by Inter-Art of London, who also
published Donald McGill's work. The girl seems
more of a 1920s flapper than a post-Edwardian
beauty.

Facing page, bottom
Beach photographers at work on the sands at
Bridlington, *c.* 1900.

LEAVE YOUR TROUBLES BEHIND AND COME TO MARGATE

Titchfield Series Copyright No. 418

HAVE JUST REACHED THIS LOVELY PLACE.

Bibliography

Much of the information collected for this book came from local seaside sources: newspapers, magazines, guide books, brochures, private diaries and letters preserved in the archives of public libraries and record offices. The authors found their best stories about Ramsgate, for instance, in a collection of articles, many of them by C. V. Horne, clipped from local newspapers and collected together by the Reference Librarian at the Ramsgate Public Library. There have also been many books published in which the British seaside has figured, and readers of this book should find the following selection interesting and entertaining.

Becker, Bernard: *Holiday Haunts* Remington, London, 1884

Bede, Cuthbert: *Mattins and Muttons* Sampson Low, London, 1866

Betjeman, John and Gray, J. S.: *Victorian and Edwardian Brighton from Old Photographs* Batsford, London, 1972

Buxton, Elizabeth Ellen: *Family Sketchbook A Hundred Years Ago* (ed. by Ellen R. C. Creighton) Geoffrey Bles, London, 1967

Carline, Richard: *Pictures in the Post* Gordon Fraser, London, 1959

Cecil, Robert: *Life in Edwardian England* Batsford, London, 1969

Eyre, Kathleen: *Bygone Blackpool* Hendon, Nelson, 1971

Gatty, Mrs Alfred (Margaret): *British Seaweeds* Bell and Daldy, London 1863

Gilbert, E. W.: *Brighton, Old Ocean's Bauble* Methuen, London, 1953

Gosse, Edmund: *Father and Son* First Edition Heinemann, London, 1907

Gosse, Philip Henry and Emily: *Sea-Side Pleasures* London, 1853

Gosse, Philip Henry: *A Year at the Shore* London, 1865

Granville, A. B.: *Spas of England and Principal Sea-Bathing Places* London, 1841. Reprinted by Adams and Dart, London, 1971

Grey, Howard and Stuart, Graham: *The Victorians by the Sea* Academy Editions, London, 1973

Holt, Tonie and Valmai: *Picture Postcards of the Golden Age* MacGibbon and Kee, London, 1971

Howell, Sarah: *The Seaside* Studio Vista, London, 1974

Lindley, Kenneth: *Seaside Architecture* Hugh Evelyn, London, 1973

Manning-Sanders, Ruth: *Seaside England* Batsford, London, 1951.

Marsden, Christopher: *The English at the Seaside* Collins, London, 1947

Martin, Paul: *Victorian Snapshots* Country Life, London, 1939

Moorhouse, Sydney: *Holiday Lancashire* Robert Hale, London, 1955

Musgrave, Clifford: *Life in Brighton* Faber and Faber, London, 1970

Pimlott, J. A. R.: *The Englishman's Holiday* Faber and Faber, London, 1947

Pope, W. Macqueen: *Twenty Shillings in the Pound* Hutchinson, London, 1948

Pulling, Christopher: *They Were Singing* Geo. G. Harrap, London, 1952

Reynolds, Harry: *Minstrel Memories* Alston Rivers, London, 1928

Round the Coast George Newnes, 1895

Stokes, H. G.: *The Very First History of the English Seaside* Sylvan Press, London, 1947

Swinglehurst, Edmund: *The Romantic Journey* Pica Editions, London, 1974

Thomson, J. H.: *Brighton: The Road, The Place, The People* London, 1862

Acknowledgments

We wish to thank the many people whose generous help and co-operation provided much of the best material in this book. We are particularly indebted to Mr and Mrs John Crowder, Mr Geoffrey Kemp, Mr Lionel Lambourne, Mr John Price, and Lady West, who kindly allowed us to reproduce material from their private collections.

The staff of many public libraries were also very helpful. Our special thanks go to the reference librarians of the Blackpool, Bridlington, Brighton, Broadstairs, Folkestone, Llandudno, Margate, Newport, Ramsgate, Scarborough, Southport and Torquay Public Libraries, the National Library of Wales at Aberystwyth and the Lancashire Public Record Office.

J.A. & E.S.

Photographs and Illustrations

The publishers wish to thank the following for their co-operation in providing photographs and illustrations:

Blackpool Public Library 91, 122, 141, 143 (inset); Bridlington Public Library 33, 47 (top), 122 (top), 123 (bottom), 155 (bottom); Brighton Public Library 14 (bottom), 17 (bottom), 131; British Library 62 (top), 67 (top); Broadstairs Public Library 59; Cook, Thomas 16 (bottom); Gray, J. S. 66 (bottom), 102 (top), 112, 130; Kemp, Geoffrey, 151; Kodak Museum 30, 80, 81, 82, 83 (top), 97 (top), 104, 107, 115, 120 (inset), 121; Lancashire Record Office 11, 68 (bottom), 118; Mansell collection 84, 92, 98 (bottom), 99 (bottom), 142-3 (bottom); National Library of Wales 25 (bottom), 42, 50-51, 52, 60-61 (bottom), 106 (top), 116 (top), 133 (top); Price, John 23, 26 (top), 29 (bottom), 132 (bottom); Radio Times Hulton Picture Library 86, 99 (top), 138-9 (bottom), 139 (inset), 147; Ramsgate Public Library 26 (bottom), 27 (top), 75, 135 (top); North Yorkshire County Library 26-7 (centre), 32, 67 (bottom), 103 (bottom), 122 (top), 125 (middle); Southport Public Library 98 (top), 117 (top), 119 (top), 125 (top), 140; Torquay Public Library 14, 27 (bottom), 53 (bottom), 69 (bottom), 119 (bottom); West, Lady 102 (bottom), 103 (top), 149, 150 (bottom).

Index